Traditional Meals

for the # Frugal Family

Delicious, Nourishing Recipes for Less

Shannon Stonger

author of *Traditionally Fermented Foods* and co-author
of *The Doable Off–Grid Homestead*

PAGE STREET
PUBLISHING CO.

PAGE STREET
PUBLISHING CO.

First published in 2020 by
Page Street Publishing Co.
27 Congress Street, Suite 105
Salem, MA 01970
www.pagestreetpublishing.com

Distributed by Macmillan, sales in Canada by The Canadian Manda Group.

24   23   22   21   20   1   2   3   4   5

ISBN-13: 978-1-62414-944-3
ISBN-10: 1-62414-944-8

Library of Congress Control Number: 2019943146

Cover and book design by Meg Baskis for Page Street Publishing Co.
Photography by Shannon Stonger

Printed and bound in China

For my eaters,
big and small;
hungry and picky.
I love you all.

Contents

Introduction

Like many who grew up eating the standard American diet, I didn't really change my habits until something big made me reconsider. That something, for me, was the birth of our first child. Filled with that common trait we new parents all seem to have—a desire to give our children better—I read and cooked and read some more. What I landed on was something that just made sense: eating like our great-grandparents; knowing where our food comes from; shunning the chemicals of the so-called green revolution; eating foods in their God-given state.

Some call this traditional foods, some call it real food; I call it the only thing that really makes sense. If you can grow it and prepare it, eat it. As we became homesteaders, growing these foods has become more and more a part of the equation. Not surprisingly, wresting food from a plot of land really clarified the question supposedly answered by endless numbers of health and nutrition books: What should we eat, anyway?

Thirteen years into this feeding-a-family gig and I now have six little eaters to nourish every single day. It's not been all grass-fed liver and perfectly golden egg yolks, however; no, it's not always been easy. Along the way, there has been a lot of trial and error and a few challenges. Picky eaters, of course, but those can be accommodated. Too much time in the kitchen is another common complaint, but that can also be remedied with proper recipes and a plan.

The biggest hurdle of all, and the one many find difficult to overcome, is making it work when you don't have an endless grocery budget. The grass-fed meats and the $10 gallons of raw milk and the organic and sprouted and soured and fermented everything . . . well, it adds up really, really fast. Especially when you're feeding a family of eight.

I am not a natural problem solver, so I struggled with this for a period of time. We made some compromises I regret, reprioritized and shifted things around when we realized we had messed up. I compared prices per nutrient—macro and micro— to really know what *food value* we were getting for our dollar. I made lists of things from the Clean Fifteen that didn't need to be organic. I compared meat prices and fat prices and bulk prices in order to know what to prioritize.

We've gone through times of having $50 to feed a family of four; $100 to feed a family of eight. That experience really taught me three things: First, cheap food is cheap for a reason and you pay for it eventually. Second, it doesn't take long for those cheap foods to impact your health. The final thing that I learned was that to nourish a family it *does* take prioritizing your time and finances . . . but it doesn't have to cost as much as you might think.

I've now found that we can feed our family of eight, with little of what I consider compromise, for an average of $280/week. According to the USDA's Official Food Plan for June 2019,[1] a family our size should be spending anywhere from $300 to $600 per week on their Thrifty to Liberal spending breakdown. It should be mentioned that we produce some of our own food, including raw milk, a portion of our meat, all of our eggs and as many vegetables as we can muster throughout the year. For that reason, I have included animal feed in the total and then padded it with an additional $25/week. By the way, that includes household items, such as diapers, toilet paper and paper towels. And we are basically feeding four adults and four children, since our oldest boys, aged eleven and thirteen, eat more than their parents most days of the week.

---

1 https://fns-prod.azureedge.net/sites/default/files/media/file/CostofFoodMay2019.pdf

Over $280/week grocery budget breaks down as follows:

- $160: Weekly groceries & household items
- $35: Average weekly total of bulk food purchases through Azure, Amazon, etc.
- $60: Weekly animal feed costs (this goes into milk and eggs and to raise meat birds and pigs)
- $25: Padding that represents homegrown eggs and produce

I should also mention that our family, like many these days, has multiple food sensitivities. These are not full-on allergies; it is simply individuals avoiding certain foods because they don't make them feel as well. These sensitivities include eggs, all pasteurized dairy and wheat. So, while those of us who tolerate them do eat plenty of our homegrown pastured eggs, I almost never cook with pasteurized dairy or wheat . . . which is why the recipes in this book are almost entirely free of those two foods.

Whether our budget seems like a lot or a little is entirely dependent on where you are coming from—both geographically and experientially. We live in an area that has a much lower cost of living than many locations; it also happens to be a bit of a black hole for organic, real food. We've also spent significantly more on groceries, per person, at various points in time when we were able to. There are so many variables and so many different circumstances that I hesitated to even share our numbers in this book. In the end, I thought it might help someone and so it is with trepidation that I share our budget.

Beyond the numbers, I wanted to share what recipes and practices have helped me the most in keeping our budget down, maintaining a nutrient-dense diet for our growing family in those most critical of years and getting everything you can out of the foods you do purchase.

The impetus for this book was born at a time when both my husband and I, homesteaders and freelancers, were in between steady work. Those months had us tightening the budget to the lowest end of the dollar range you read and forced us to get extra creative. It also taught me quite a bit about the things we don't need to buy, the inexpensive whole foods that truly nourish us and the recipes we could eat over and over again, even when the budget loosens up. My hope is that this book will help and inspire you to nourish your family, even in the leanest of times.

Shannon Stonger

Making Traditional Foods Work on a Budget

Defining Traditional Foods

The traditional foods movement has garnered a fair amount of attention in the last couple of decades, and along with that attention has come a number of variations and definitions. Real food is most often synonymous with traditional food but other ideas, such as Paleo and Keto, have taken hold of groups of those tending toward traditional foods.

Defining traditional food is like defining sustainability; there really is no one right answer. But for a book that is filled with recipes I am calling traditional foods recipes, I figure I'd better share my own definition.

I see traditional foods as those foods that have been eaten by people groups for generations. Not only that, these people groups have thrived and sustained good health on these foods. The foods are usually very simple, unadulterated by modern industrialism—both in farming and in processing—and are considered nutrient-dense.

Weston A. Price, and the foundation of the same name, is often cited as a sort of inspiration for this type of diet, yet I have found that the simple answers he found have been either skewed or ignored altogether. My understanding of his work is that, as a dentist, he desired in the 1920s to prove a hypothesis he'd come up with concerning modern diets and the damage they were doing: that animal products were a possible culprit and that if he traveled to remote locations throughout the world, he would find healthy cultures living on preindustrial foods that were devoid of animal products.

What he found flew in the face of that hypothesis, but only to a certain degree. Not a single healthy, thriving people group avoided the consumption of animal products. Rather, these people revered animal foods for their health-giving properties, often putting a great deal of effort into procuring or raising them themselves. Seafood and dairy for the Irish, rich golden dairy products in the Alps, organ meats and milk in Africa—these were the foods most prized in these regions.

But these foods were not all in plenty, a fact that made them all the more valuable. No, oftentimes these foods made up a small percentage of daily calories, but calories that packed a punch with fat-soluble vitamins and other nutrients harder to get from plant foods.

So, instead of omitting animal products and the saturated fats they often contain, traditional foods embrace high-quality animal foods fed on pasture and little to no grain. Simple foods, such as broth and eggs and fermented vegetables and greens, are everyday pieces of the traditional foods dietary puzzle.

Grains are soaked, soured or sprouted to unlock their nourishing potential. The same goes for seeds and legumes, some of the most nutritious and inexpensive foods you can purchase. Seasonal vegetables are emphasized and fruit is enjoyed, in season. Meals are simple fare, and always homemade. Creative combinations that come from those inspiring ingredients make the food often greater than the sum of its parts, something you find when you travel or embrace food cultures from around the world.

Most of all, traditional foods are those that have been eaten, and often grown, for generations by those who desire to feel well. They also just happen to taste really good and come together without too much fuss.

One of the simplest ways to define traditional foods is to simply eat how our great great grandparents did, before the advent of the supermarket and industrial agriculture.

The Frugal Traditional Foods Shopping List

If you're like me, you get to a pantry list in a cookbook and you just keep flipping the pages. You've seen one list, you've seen them all, right? For that reason, I hesitated to put these lists together. Then again, I realized I would have liked to have had these lists a decade ago.

You see, I have spent years comparing nutrition, prices and quality in my grocery shopping. At first, it was in the brick-and-mortar grocery stores and the farmers' markets. Then, I looked into Amazon and Azure Standard, Thrive Market and Vitacost. All the while, I wanted to know one thing: How can we get the most nutrients first, calories second, for the best deal? How can we keep organic in mind much of the time while keeping our budget under $300 per week for a family of eight? How can we fit in the raw dairy and the seasonal vegetables and the high-quality proteins without breaking the bank?

You might be wondering why I choose the items I do in each category. Good cheese is really expensive so I either make my own or we drink raw milk and kefir.

The seed grains—buckwheat, amaranth and quinoa—are easy to digest and make great porridge or side dishes.

We tend to eat from the Clean Fifteen list while utilizing homegrown or organic store-bought produce for the vegetables with a heavier pesticide load. We also try to limit fruit intake, out of season, as that can add a lot of dollar signs to the budget.

Eventually, this list became how I shopped. It contains the best deals in its category, both at price per pound and nutrients per pound. I also order the headings of this list (grains, dairy, etc.) according to the importance I place on them in prioritizing my budget. So, since raw dairy is so important to me for the health of our children, I spend money on that first. Grains, beans and root vegetables, because they provide a bulk of calories, come next, and so on.

Rather than being a list of all the foods that would be good to have in each category, this list is pared down to the items I buy regularly to stay within budget. They are things you would see on my list every single week or every single bulk order.

All eggs and dairy are locally raised (by us or neighbors) and are grass-fed. All grains, flours, legumes and seeds we purchase in 25- or 50-pound (11.3- or 22.7-kg) bags from Azure Standard. The meat and produce are split between whatever we can grow ourselves organically and whatever we can source from my two local grocery stores, Aldi and Walmart. Fats are a combination of bulk 5-gallon (19-L) purchases (expeller-pressed coconut oil), homemade raw butter and small bottles of organic olive or avocado oil purchased here and there.

In the category of legumes, I prefer lentils and chickpeas because they meet my criteria for easiest to sprout, most versatile and cheapest per pound. We do eat pinto and black beans, from time to time, as well. Nuts and nut butters are a treat food for us since I find bulk chia and sunflower seeds to have the most bang for our buck.

Eggs & Dairy

- Raw milk
- Raw milk made into kefir
- Truly pastured eggs

Gluten-Free Grains & Flours

- Buckwheat, groats and flour
- Oats, rolled and flour
- Sorghum, grain and flour
- White & brown basmati or jasmine rice
- Organic masa (corn) flour
- Amaranth grain
- Quinoa grain
- Tapioca starch
- Potato starch

Legumes

- Dried lentils
- Dried chickpeas
- Other dried beans

Clean Conventional Produce

- Cabbages
- Onions
- Avocados
- Frozen broccoli
- Sweet potatoes
- Frozen wild blueberries
- Garlic

Frugal Organic Produce

- Carrots
- Celery
- Potatoes
- Bananas
- Seasonal fruit (when the price gets low)
- Seasonal vegetables (when the price gets low)

Traditional Fats

- Expeller-pressed coconut oil
- Raw grass-fed butter (homemade)
- Organic olive or avocado oil

Pastured & Wild Proteins

I know it is often advised to buy meat with bones in it, but I have actually found it more economical to seek out bones from a local farmer or butcher and buy them in bulk, and make huge batches of broth.

- Bones for making broth
- Grass-fed ground beef
- Canned wild Alaskan salmon
- Whole pastured chickens
- Offal

Seeds & Nuts

- Raw sunflower seed kernels
- Chia seeds
- Shredded unsweetened coconut
- Tahini in bulk

Other

- Apple cider vinegar
- Bulk Himalayan pink salt
- Bulk spices

Anything we can buy in bulk, usually from Azure Standard, we do. But we also do a weekly grocery run.

A Sample of My Weekly Grocery Shopping

To give you an idea of what I really buy and what that looks like financially, here is a typical week's worth of grocery purchases. This is indicative of a winter grocery shop when fresh produce is not available locally.

- 4 cabbages
- 6 pounds (2.7 kg) frozen broccoli
- 5 pounds (2.3 kg) grass-fed ground meat
- 4 large cans wild Alaskan salmon
- 4 bunches organic bananas
- 10 pounds (4.5 kg) grapefruit (in season)
- 2 bags yellow onions
- 3 heads fresh garlic
- 2 large cans organic diced tomatoes
- 6 small cans tomato sauce
- 14 small avocados
- 2 pounds (905 g) organic carrots
- 5 pounds (2.3 kg) basmati rice
- 6 cans coconut milk
- 5 pounds (4.5 kg) frozen wild blueberries
- 1 bunch each cilantro and parsley
- Paper towels, diapers, toilet paper
- Animal feed (alfalfa cubes that we feed our milk cow and goats for raw milk, and local clean-out grain that we feed to our laying hens and meat birds and pigs)

This is supplemented by the bulk grains, beans, flours, seeds and coconut oil we purchase, which amounts to about $35/week.

What I Don't Buy

These are particularly pricey, especially good-quality products, so we only buy them as rare treats.

- Lunch or processed meats
- Breads or any baked goods
- Nuts or nut butters
- Organic vegetables out of season (bell peppers, zucchini, eggplant, tomatoes, etc.)
- Canned beans, fruits or vegetables (though we do can our own)
- Packaged seasoning mix, premade sauces, cereals, granolas, etc.

What We Buy Organic and What We Don't

If you're like me, you have to set priorities. Sure, we'd like to eat 100 percent organic, but that's not always feasible. So, when that happens, it is time to prioritize.

We mostly buy pasture-raised and organic animal products. We mostly buy organic grains and beans, due to the glyphosate used in the production of these foods. We buy organic white potatoes, unless we grow those ourselves. We buy organic oils and fats. We buy organic lettuces and greens.

We buy conventional cabbages, broccoli, avocados, Brussels sprouts, sweet potatoes, onions, citrus, wild blueberries, coconut milk and rice. We buy conventional sunflower and chia seeds, unless we can get organic at a similar price to conventional. We mix and match organic and conventional tomato products, depending on the week.

As for animal feed, we buy local grain that is non-GMO but not certified organic. We use this to supplement the kitchen scraps, skim milk, eggs and pasture grasses we feed our own chickens, pigs, goats and cows.

At least, that is what we do *most* of the time. If things are tighter than usual, we start making tough decisions.

It's not perfect, not by a long shot, but it works for us and I'm mostly comfortable with it. That's not to say we don't consider upping the grocery budget from time to time, especially as our children grow older and hungrier. But I am thankful for options that allow us to prioritize what we need and make some compromises on those things less important.

Fitting Diverse Dietary Restrictions into the Budget

So, one of you is gluten-free and one can't eat eggs and he can't have cheese, and you are on Keto, there are a couple of picky toddlers in the mix and we need to stick to what grocery budget, exactly? Yeah, planning meals can feel like skiing down a thickly forested mountain, with more bobbing and weaving than those times you're trying to make it through the checkout line at the grocery store with a screaming baby. I know; we've been there, too.

You feel like this is impossible, the act of feeding everyone what they need without becoming a short-order cook and completely breaking the budget. But it's not. Here are a few things I've learned.

- Find foods that everyone can come together around. Everyone can eat vegetables, broth and meat in our family, so most of our meals revolve around those foods. If we are adding potatoes or rice to these foods as they are cooking, I take out a little of the veggies and meat and set them aside for someone on Keto.

- Add carbs for those who eat them; supplement with something simple for those who can't. For growing children, I strongly disagree with any sort of macronutrient restriction, save the rare exception like that a Keto diet is needful for medical reasons. Let them eat fat and carbs and protein, as long as these have clean sources, is my theory. So, most of our meals involve a pot of soaked grains or white rice; white or sweet potatoes; beans or a loaf of gluten-free bread. Those who can partake do, and for those who don't, I'll throw on an avocado or a simple fried egg or a much larger salad (my giant dinner salads are oddly comical to my children).

- Get rid of expensive foods that not everyone can eat. For us, cheese and peanut or almond butters are things we purchase maybe a couple of times a year. We really like these foods, but they are really expensive and we can make up those calories and nutrients elsewhere.

- Cook with the frugal eaters in mind. If someone in your family is cutting carbs or has another more expensive dietary need than the rest, that is the person you cook a separate meal for. The majority of our family can eat inexpensive grains and beans regularly, so long as they are prepared well.

- Be prepared for snacks but don't encourage them. One thing I have long worked towards is eliminating snacking all together. This works with some of my children, but some of them can easily out eat their parents and still be hungry two hours later, even with loads of good fat at the meal. So, I try to have something they can eat, but something inexpensive. The category of snack foods is where things really add up, so serve them foods you don't normally find in that category. Snacks in our house are usually whatever seasonal fruit we have around, a big glass of fresh milk, or leftovers from a previous meal.

• Navigating various food allergies or sensitivities can be tough, especially when you are also working within a certain budget and have other parameters to consider. This particular challenge is actually the motivation behind this book and my hope is that my struggles might bring you solutions.

About Ingredients

I know we all want to utilize the cleanest, highest-quality ingredients we can . . . but we also have to be mindful of the budget. Over the years, I have come to use specific ingredients that I find to be a good balance between high quality and economical. These are ingredients I use nearly every single day and are called for throughout the recipes in this book. The following are the versions of these products I use or recommend using.

Salt: Generally three varieties of salt are made mention of when you research the traditional foods' take on the topic. Celtic sea salt, Himalayan pink salt and Redmond Real Salt are all touted as options with many authors or medical professionals having a personal preference. There is some concern over sea salt and the microplastics contained therein. Of the three, I find Himalayan pink salt to be the most economical per pound and it is therefore the variety I use in all of my recipes.

Water: Tap water from treated city water may contain chlorine and fluoride, which can often hamper fermentation, and some do not want to consume these halogens due to health concerns. For that reason, many find that filtering their water is the safest bet. We happen to utilize rain water for all of our household cooking and cleaning and therefore filter it before drinking, using a Berkey water filter.

Apple cider vinegar: This is a staple in our home, for use in salad dressings as well as for adding to beverages to aid digestion. We prefer one that is both raw and organic. Bragg is a popular and widely available brand, but we have also purchased other brands from Walmart or Azure and have found no difference in quality.

Honey: A local, raw variety from bees that aren't being kept near industrial agriculture is probably your best option when it comes to sourcing honey. This is an expensive ingredient and one that I like to use sparingly, added as a sweetener after baking instead of killing the enzymes through baking, for instance. Lower-priced honey—or coconut sugar—is what we use for baking in our home.

Milk: Any recipe that calls for milk was tested with raw whole milk from our family milk cow or full-fat coconut milk, as indicated.

Produce: Potatoes, strawberries, greens, carrots, celery, apples and most other fruits called for in the recipes are organic, due to high pesticide residues. Such vegetables as broccoli, onions, avocados and cabbage that are called for frequently are less of a concern, and so are generally conventional.

Baking powder: We always look for an aluminum-free baking powder, which is more economical when purchased in bulk. You can also make a very frugal homemade baking powder which you can find on the Nourishing Days blog.

A word of encouragement: Be careful not to compare what you are able to do with where someone else is at. Do what you can with what you have and improve as your knowledge and resources increase.

Thrifty Mornings

Before the bustle of school, work and animal chores, breakfast begins. It has to be substantial enough to get us through the work of the morning with even energy. It has to be simple enough for me to get cooking, bleary-eyed between sips of coffee, while the house is still quiet. It has to feed a small army, nourish growing bodies and not cost an arm and a leg. The recipes in this chapter are my answer to that.

Dairy, eggs and soaked or sprouted grains make up the bulk of the breakfasts we eat and the recipes you will find in this chapter. Gluten-free "seed grains," such as buckwheat and amaranth, are some of our favorites and are made into porridge (page 35), a breakfast cake (page 31) and a big fruit- and seed-filled breakfast bake (page 39).

Eggs are a simple, nourishing start to any day. We like to eat them fried, scrambled and cooked up in a one-pan skillet with sweet potatoes and greens (page 24).

I had long since given up on cold cereal, devoid of much in the way of calories or nutrition and a budget buster to boot. But something about a cold bowl of milk and a crunchy, truly nutritious, grain cereal propelled me into experimentation. Having tried many soaked granolas over the years, I knew something different needed to be done. Something less like a giant graham cracker you have to break up and more like a real-deal granola. Two of those recipes can be found in this chapter (pages 18 and 28), one of which is based on buckwheat rather than oats.

And I could not write a breakfast chapter that didn't include pancakes (page 27). My children just love a good stack of pancakes with butter and raw honey melting down the sides.

All of these are family favorites from over the years, enjoyed as a family of four, six and now eight. They have stood the test of time or come as brand-new revelations to our morning meal, and I hope you enjoy them as much as we do.

A Better Kefir-Chia Soaked Granola

About ten years ago, I came across the concept of soaking granola before baking it. Most of the recipes are very similar and result in a hard-to-make, hard-to-chew cross between a granola and a dehydrated bread product. After years of giving up on the stuff, I decided to throw out those recipes and start over. The result is a granola that actually tastes light and crisp, like the real deal, but with all the benefits of soaking. Note that you can omit the honey all together, without changing the texture of the granola, if you are avoiding sweeteners.

Makes
20 servings

9 cups (720 g) rolled oats, gluten-free, if needed

½ cup (80 g) chia seeds

2½ cups (590 ml) Milk Kefir (page 146)

3 cups (435 g) raw sunflower seeds or any combination of whole, raw seeds or nuts

1 tbsp (18 g) sea salt for granola, plus 1 tsp for soaking the seeds

1 tbsp (14 g) coconut oil, for baking pans

1 cup (240 ml) melted coconut oil or unsalted butter

1 cup (340 g) raw honey

2 tsp (10 ml) vanilla extract

2 tbsp (14 g) ground cinnamon

3 cups (255 g) unsweetened shredded coconut

3 cups (450 g) dried fruit of choice (optional)

Raw milk, kefir, yogurt or diluted coconut milk, for serving

At least a full 24 hours before you plan to bake the granola, in a very large bowl, stir together the oats and chia seeds until evenly distributed. Pour in the milk kefir and mix, first with a wooden spoon and then with your hands, until all the oats and seeds are moistened by the kefir. Be careful not to compact the oats together too much while you are stirring. The mixture will not be terribly wet, but there will be a bit of moisture so that everything gets enough contact with the kefir for fermentation.

Cover the bowl with a lid or plastic wrap and leave it to soak in a warm place in your kitchen for at least 24 hours. You can go as long as 48 hours for a bit more tang.

Meanwhile, in a 2-quart (1.9-L) vessel, combine your sunflower seeds with water to cover and add 1 teaspoon of the salt. Leave the seeds to soak for the duration of the oat-soaking period.

Once the soaking period is up, preheat the oven to 275°F (140°C) and lightly grease 3 half-sheet baking pans with coconut oil.

Uncover the soaked oat mixture; it will be quite stiff, having absorbed all the liquid. Break it up into clumps with a sturdy wooden spoon. Drain the sunflower seeds very well (discard the salted water) and then add them to the broken-up oat mixture.

Pour in the melted coconut oil, honey, tablespoon (18 g) of salt, vanilla and cinnamon. Add the shredded coconut and stir the whole lot together with a spoon, being careful not to compact it, until everything is completely combined.

Divide the oat mixture among the 3 half-sheet baking pans. Spread out the mixture into an even layer, being careful not to press too much.

(Continued)

A Better Kefir-Chia Soaked Granola *(Continued)*

Bake for 30 minutes. Remove the pans from the oven, stir the granola mixture, using 2 forks, then return the pans to the oven, rotating their positions in the oven. Bake for an additional 30 minutes, stir again and rotate the pans' oven position, then repeat 2 more times, for a total bake time of 2 hours.

At this point, the granola ought to be golden brown and the oats should feel dry to the touch. If they are still a bit pale or moist, return them to the oven for an additional 10 to 15 minutes of baking, as needed.

Once the granola is fully baked, remove from the oven, sprinkle the dried fruits over the warm granola and allow everything to cool to room temperature. As it cools, the granola will crisp up. Once fully cooled, transfer it to an airtight container, where it should keep for several weeks.

Serve the granola with raw milk, kefir, yogurt or diluted coconut milk.

Making Soaking, Sprouting and Souring Easy and Efficient

I often have jars and bowls of all sorts of living things on my kitchen counter that need my attention daily. Soaking beans, sprouting seeds, culturing milk kefir, bubbling sourdough, soaking grains . . . boy, it can be a lot to keep up with sometimes.

At first I wanted to give up; it just felt like too much. Eventually, though, I realized it was necessary for our health and our budget, so I decided that instead of giving up, I would try to find ways to simplify it. Now, I am not a super-type-A organizing freak; quite the opposite, actually. No, for me to make this simple was not going to involve extensive planning or list making.

Instead, I break things up into daily and weekly kitchen chores. Every day, I work with the kefir and any other ferments I have going. If I am sprouting, I add rinsing those to my mental list of daily kitchen jobs. I keep the sprout jars next to the water filter to remind me of this task. It really just takes a few minutes.

I also plan to get some things soaking a couple of times per week, often quickly throwing beans or grains in with water and then planning meals from there. So, I decide what I am going to soak and then cook from there. In other words, I might start a pot of chickpeas and a bowl of A Better Kefir-Chia Soaked Granola (page 18) soaking on Monday along with a double batch of Soaked Gluten-Free Artisan Bread (page 88). That ensures that by Tuesday, we'll have bread; and by Wednesday or Thursday, we will have enough chickpeas soaking for a batch of both falafel (page 47) and hummus (page 91).

Then on Thursday, I get a few more things soaking—say, buckwheat for a breakfast cake (page 31), lentils for a lentil and rice bake (page 56) and a couple of bowls of flour (since mixing two is as easy as mixing one) for pancakes (page 27) and a weekend treat of Sweet Potato Chocolate Cake (page 119).

This works much better for me, personally, then meticulously planning things out. It also works well because I know if I get something soaking, we will have food in a couple of days. Furthermore, I don't have to know exactly what I am making three days ahead of time; I can cross that bridge when I come to it and mix up the grains and beans with whatever produce we have coming from our garden.

Soaked 100% Rolled Oat Pancakes

When we had a 50-pound (22.7-kg) bag of rolled oats, I needed to come up with something besides oatmeal to make with them. These delicious pancakes were the result. What I love about them is that, unlike most pancakes, these keep the hungry little ones full for hours. Besides being extra-hearty, the marriage of oats, cinnamon and vanilla just sings when topped with butter and syrup or nut butter and jam.

Serves

4

1½ cups (120 g) rolled oats, gluten-free, if needed

½ cup (120 ml) warm water, about 110°F (43°C)

¼ cup (60 ml) kefir, or coconut milk + 1 tbsp (15 ml) apple cider vinegar

3 large, pasture-raised eggs, beaten

2 tsp (9 g) baking powder

Pinch of salt

1 tbsp (20 g) raw honey

1½ tsp (4 g) ground cinnamon

1 tsp vanilla extract

Coconut oil or unsalted butter, for cooking

Butter, nut butter, jam, honey or pure maple syrup, for serving

The day before you wish to serve the pancakes for breakfast, in a medium-sized bowl (narrow seems to work better), combine the oats, warm water and kefir. Mix well, mashing the oats down into the liquid as much as possible. Leave in a warm place for 12 to 24 hours.

In the morning, heat a skillet over medium-low heat.

In a small bowl, combine the eggs, baking powder, salt, honey, cinnamon and vanilla. Pour the egg mixture into the oat mixture and stir to incorporate. It will be thick, unlike regular pancake batter.

Melt the coconut oil in the warm skillet. For each pancake, scoop a heaping tablespoon (16 g) or two (32 g) of batter into your skillet. Gently spread the batter until ¹⁄₁₆ to ⅛ inch (1.5 to 3 mm) thick.

Allow to cook until the bottom has set and the edges and top begin to dry out, 4 to 5 minutes. Flip and allow to cook for another 3 minutes or so.

Serve warm with butter, nut butter, jam, honey or maple syrup.

Sweet Potato & Greens Breakfast Skillet

In the winter, after our sweet potatoes have had a chance to cure, this hearty farm breakfast is perfect for a slow morning or breakfast for dinner. Play around with it by adding a sweet (or hot!) pepper or replacing the sweet potatoes with white potatoes. If you are making this for someone who cannot eat eggs, use the optional sausage as an alternative protein.

Serves
4

¼ cup (55 g) lard, coconut oil or ghee

1 large onion, diced

1 lb (455 g) bulk sausage (optional)

4 medium-sized sweet potatoes, diced

2 bunches collard or kale greens, stems removed, chopped

8 large, pasture-raised eggs

Fruit or Soaked Gluten-Free Artisan Bread (page 88), for serving

In a large skillet over medium heat, melt the lard. Add the onion and cook for 4 to 6 minutes, or until the onion is translucent. If using sausage instead of eggs, add that to the pan and cook for 8 to 10 minutes, or until well browned.

Add the sweet potatoes and greens and stir everything together. Partially cover the pan with a lid. Cook, stirring occasionally, for 10 to 15 minutes, or until the sweet potatoes are tender.

Use the back of a spoon to create 8 small wells throughout the mixture in the pan. Crack the eggs in the wells and place the lid on the pan. Cook, covered, for 5 to 8 minutes, or until the whites are set and the yolks are cooked to your liking.

Dish up 2 eggs and a generous scoop of vegetables per serving. Serve alongside fresh fruit or Soaked Gluten-Free Artisan Bread.

The Best Grain-Free Pancakes

Originally from the Nourishing Days blog, this is easily the most popular recipe on the site. It is also one of the more fickle recipes I've created, as it can go wrong with just a small change in measurement or ingredient substitution. This updated version includes the option of adding just a little bit of potato starch to the mixture, which makes the pancakes even better. But prepare them as in the original recipe, with just coconut flour, for a low-carb treat.

Serves

4

4 large, pasture-raised eggs, at room temperature

¾ cup (175 ml) heavy cream + ¼ cup (60 ml) whole milk (best), 1 cup (240 ml) coconut milk or ¾ cup (173 g) whole-milk yogurt + ¼ cup (60 ml) whole milk

2 tsp (10 ml) vanilla extract

½ cup minus 1 tbsp (49 g) coconut flour + ¼ cup (37 g) potato starch (see Note)

2 tsp (9 g) baking powder

¼ tsp sea salt

Coconut oil or unsalted butter, for griddle

Butter, coconut oil, honey, pure maple syrup or fruit, for serving

Heat a griddle over medium-low heat.

In a small bowl, beat the eggs until frothy, about 2 minutes. Mix in the milk mixture and vanilla.

In a medium-sized bowl, whisk together the coconut flour (and potato starch, if using), baking powder and salt. Stir the wet mixture into the dry until everything is well incorporated. Allow to sit for 3 to 5 minutes. At this stage, your batter should be thick, almost like brownie batter.

Oil the griddle with coconut oil. Ladle a few tablespoons (about 30 ml) of batter into the pan for each pancake. Spread out slightly with the back of a spoon. The pancakes should be 2 to 3 inches (5 to 7.5 cm) in diameter and fairly thick. Cook for a few minutes on each side, or until the tops dry out slightly and the bottoms start to brown. Flip and cook for an additional 2 to 3 minutes.

Serve hot with butter, coconut oil, honey, maple syrup or fruit.

Note: The original recipe, while less like fluffy diner pancakes, is still delicious and is completely low carb. For that version, simply omit the potato starch and use a full ½ cup (56 g) of coconut flour.

Activated Buckwheat Cereal

Cold cereal is one of those things you can really miss when you move away from processed foods. Besides the Better Kefir–Chia Soaked Granola (page 18), this recipe is our family's favorite way to fill that void. Buckwheat, because it is actually more of a seed than a grain, is often more easily tolerated than oats by those with digestive issues. However, activating —another term for soaking or sprouting—the seed gives it even more benefit. All that healthy stuff aside, this recipe is just really tasty with some cold raw milk or coconut milk. You will find directions for soaking the buckwheat on page 143, but if you have an extra day or so, you can continue that soaking process and actually sprout the buckwheat before mixing up the granola.

Makes
15 servings

4 cups (680 g) raw buckwheat groats (not toasted)

2 cups (290 g) raw sunflower seeds

2 tbsp (28 g) coconut oil, for baking sheets

⅓ cup (80 ml) melted coconut oil or unsalted butter

¼ cup (40 g) chia seeds

1 cup (85 g) unsweetened coconut flakes

½ cup (170 g) honey, preferably raw

2 tsp (12 g) salt

1 tsp vanilla extract

2 tsp (5 g) ground cinnamon

2 cups (300 g) dried fruit (optional)

Place the buckwheat groats in a half-gallon (2-L) jar or similarly sized bowl. Fill the jar with water, leaving ½ inch (1.3 cm) of space. Place the sunflower seeds in a quart-sized (1-L) jar and fill the jar with water, leaving ½ inch (1.3 cm) of space. Cover both jars loosely with a plastic lid or canning lid and ring. Leave on the counter to soak for 12 to 24 hours. Alternatively, you can sprout the buckwheat by following the tutorial on page 143.

After the soaking period is up, preheat your oven to 300°F (150°C) and lightly grease 2 baking sheets with the 2 tablespoons (28 g) of coconut oil or line them with parchment paper.

Drain the buckwheat and rinse it really well to remove the mucilaginous liquid that forms during soaking. Drain the sunflower seeds and transfer both the buckwheat and the sunflower seeds to a large bowl. Add the melted coconut oil, chia seeds, coconut flakes, honey, salt, vanilla and cinnamon, and mix everything really well with a wooden spoon until the mixture is homogenous.

Transfer the mixture to the prepared baking sheets and spread it out evenly, pressing down lightly with the back of a spoon or spatula to compact the granola into clusters. Bake for 30 minutes. Remove from the oven, stir around using 2 forks and place back in the oven, rotating the pan positions. Bake for an additional 20 minutes, stir again and bake for an additional 10 to 20 minutes, for a total of 60 to 70 minutes, or until golden and the buckwheat and seeds are dry, but not completely hardened.

Remove from the oven and sprinkle the dried fruit right onto the granola mixture. Let cool completely before storing for up to a week at room temperature or 2 weeks in the refrigerator.

Soaked Buckwheat Breakfast Cake

At some point, I realized that making pancakes for six hungry children was much less efficient than throwing that batter into a pan and baking it while I did something else. Thus the "breakfast cake" was born. This version is made with our favorite single-grain gluten-free flour, but feel free to sub in whatever your favorites are. We like to save our sweetener of choice—raw honey—for drizzling just before serving to retain all of those good enzymes, rather than baking it into the cake.

Serves
8 to 10

3 cups (360 g) buckwheat flour

2½ cups (590 ml) Milk Kefir (page 146), or (460 g) dairy or nondairy yogurt

⅓ cup (55 g) + 2 tbsp (28 g) coconut oil, for baking pan

5 large, pasture-raised eggs

1 tbsp (7 g) ground cinnamon

1 tsp salt

1½ tbsp (21 g) baking powder

Yogurt, kefir, raw or dairy-free milk, honey and fruit, for serving

In a large bowl, combine the buckwheat flour and milk kefir to form a thick batter, cover with a lid or plastic wrap and allow to soak for 12 to 24 hours.

The next morning, preheat the oven to 350°F (180°C) and generously grease a 9 x 13–inch (23 x 33–cm) baking pan with 2 tablespoons (28 g) of coconut oil.

Crack the eggs into the soaked buckwheat mixture and add the remaining coconut oil, cinnamon and salt. Stir until it is mostly mixed and then sprinkle with the baking powder. Stir until all the ingredients are combined.

Transfer the batter to the prepared baking pan and smooth out the top with a spatula. Bake for 35 to 45 minutes, or until a cake tester inserted into the center comes out clean.

Remove from the oven and allow to cool for at least 5 minutes before serving. To serve, top with yogurt, kefir, raw or dairy-free milk along with honey and fruit, as desired.

Notes: For an egg-free version that won't have quite as much lift, replace the eggs with 1 cup (225 g) of mashed banana mixed with 2 tablespoons (14 g) of ground flaxseed.

If you do not like the supernutty flavor of buckwheat, substitute sorghum flour for half of the volume of the buckwheat flour.

Greek Fauxgurt

It is impossible to make this recipe dairy-free—the only recipe in the book without a dairy-free option! But if you can tolerate good, raw dairy, this recipe is such a winner. Store-bought cottage cheese needs no added cream, so omit if necessary. When my children tire of the endless supply of cottage cheese we make from our own cow's milk, I serve this up and they love how it tastes just like thick, rich Greek yogurt!

Serves
6 to 8

1 qt (1 kg) low-fat cultured cottage cheese, preferably raw

2 cups (475 ml) grass-fed heavy cream, preferably raw, or coconut milk (omit if using a creamy, store-bought cottage cheese)

1 lb (455 g) frozen or fresh fruit, any combination

Additional fruit or seeds, for serving (optional)

In a food processor or blender, combine all three ingredients and blend until thick and smooth. Serve topped with additional fruit or seeds . . . or freeze into ice pops for a rich frozen treat.

The Dairy Question

While most of the recipes in this book are dairy free, our family consumes a good amount of raw milk, raw milk kefir and raw milk cheeses (when I make them) on a daily basis. But I rarely cook with dairy, the exception being some of the baked goods in this book that use milk kefir as a fermentation medium.

The thing about dairy is that a lot of people don't tolerate it well and, even if you can tolerate it, you need to be picky about what you consume. This is what our family looks for in fresh milk:

Milk from a local farm selling fresh, unpasteurized, unhomogenized milk. Ask to see their milking operation and look for cleanliness and good maintenance practices.

Find out what those cows or goats are fed. You want as much fresh green grass going into that animal as possible. A little grain at milking time and hay fed in winter is normal, so long as those animals see good pasture the rest of the year. A dairy animal fed on fresh green grass will produce milk rich in beneficial fatty acids and fat-soluble vitamins, which is precisely what growing children need.

Finally, ask your farmer if the cow has been tested as A2/A2. Studies have found that when consuming A1 milk, the body produces a protein fragment which has been linked to digestive, mood and neurological disorders. The mutation has only been found in cow's milk, probably due to questionable breeding practices, so goat's milk is generally considered safe.

Cream of Amaranth-Chia Porridge

In our home, porridge is not necessarily synonymous with oats. We also make porridge from buckwheat, quinoa, millet and amaranth, as in this creamy bowl. I grew up eating—and loving!—cream of wheat. This facsimile of my childhood bowl of comfort works great with simple amaranth grain due to its teeny-tiny size. It cooks up smooth and creamy and tastes a lot like those bowls of my youth when served with milk, butter and fruit or honey.

Serves
4 to 6

2 cups (350 g) dried amaranth grain (not flour)

4 cups (946 ml) water

½ cup (80 g) chia seeds

½ tsp salt

Milk, butter, fruit, sweetener, nuts, nut butter or your favorite porridge toppings, for serving

At least 12 and up to 48 hours before you plan to serve this dish, in a medium-sized saucepan, combine the amaranth, water and chia. Stir really well—you will be surprised how much you have to work at this, due to the size of the amaranth grain and its propensity for floating to the top. Leave this to soak, covered, on your kitchen counter.

In the morning, add the salt and place the pot over medium-high heat. Bring to a boil and then lower the heat so it is just simmering. Cook, stirring occasionally, for 10 to 15 minutes, or until the amaranth begins to absorb the water and thickens up. Amaranth cooks up unlike other grains, in that instead of gradually absorbing water and getting slightly thicker over time, it seems to happen all at once toward the end of this cooking process, so be aware.

Once the amaranth has a creamy, thick consistency, remove it from the heat and divide the porridge among 4 to 6 bowls. Add milk, butter, fruit, sweetener, nuts, nut butter or your favorite porridge toppings and serve piping hot.

Soaked Gluten-Free, Dairy-Free Pancakes (with an egg-free option)

Years ago, I made some gluten-free, allergen-friendly pancakes from a recipe I found. They were good but not exactly what I was looking for at the time, so I kind of filed the recipe away and forgot about it. Years later, I found and reworked the recipe and these pancakes are now a family favorite that everyone can eat. And they taste like real-deal diner pancakes, to boot!

Serves
4 to 6

¾ cup (90 g) garbanzo flour

2¼ cups (241 g) sorghum flour

1 cup (152 g) potato starch

2¼ cups (535 ml) milk, or
1¼ cups (295 ml) coconut milk +
1 cup (240 ml) water, for
dairy-free

1 tbsp (15 ml) apple cider vinegar
or kefir

2 large, pasture-raised eggs

2 tbsp (30 ml) melted coconut oil
or unsalted butter

1 tsp sea salt

1½ tsp (2 g) ground psyllium
husk

4 tsp (18 g) baking powder

Coconut oil or unsalted butter,
for cooking

Your favorite pancake toppings,
for serving

In a medium-sized bowl, combine the garbanzo flour, sorghum flour and potato starch, and whisk well. Pour in the milk and vinegar, then whisk well again to incorporate. Cover the bowl and leave the mixture to soak for 12 to 24 hours.

When ready to cook, heat a griddle over medium-high heat.

Uncover the bowl and give the mixture a whisk (you will notice a bit of separation happening between the liquid and the flours; this is normal). Crack in the eggs and add the melted coconut oil and salt. Whisk well. Sprinkle in the psyllium and baking powder and whisk it all together.

Grease your griddle lightly with coconut oil. Ladle ⅓ cup (80 ml) of the batter at a time onto the hot griddle. Cook for 3 to 4 minutes, or until the pancakes begin to dry up around the edges and bubbles are forming. Carefully flip and cook for an additional 2 to 3 minutes, or until golden brown. Repeat with the remaining batter.

Serve with your favorite pancake toppings.

Note: For egg-free pancakes, omit the eggs and substitute 2 tablespoons (14 g) of flaxseed or chia meal mixed with ½ cup (123 g) of pure pumpkin puree or ½ cup (112 g) of mashed banana. These won't be quite as fluffy as the egg-rich pancakes, but are still delicious.

Fruit & Seed Soaked Baked Buckwheat

Buckwheat is a wholesome seed grain (not technically a grain) and unrelated to wheat, so very digestible and gluten-free. Soaking buckwheat, along with seeds, turns it into a powerhouse breakfast when baked up with fruit and spices. Skipping the sweetener in the baking allows the enzymes of the raw honey to stay intact when drizzling it over just before serving.

Serves

6 to 8

2 cups (340 g) raw buckwheat groats

½ cup (73 g) sunflower seeds

½ cup (70 g) pumpkin seeds

Coconut oil or unsalted butter, for baking pan

4 large, pasture-raised eggs

2½ cups (590 ml) kefir, or 1½ cups (355 ml) coconut milk + 1 cup (240 ml) water + 1 tbsp (15 ml) apple cider vinegar

2 tsp (5 g) ground cinnamon

1 tsp sea salt

½ tsp freshly grated nutmeg

2 cups (150 g) diced fruit (apples, peaches, etc.)

Raw honey, for serving

Yogurt or fresh milk, for serving

The day before you wish to bake, soak the buckwheat groats, sunflower and pumpkin seeds. Rinse the buckwheat groats and place them in a medium-sized bowl along with the seeds. Add 5 cups (1.2 L) of water, cover and leave to soak for 12 to 24 hours.

When you are ready to bake, preheat the oven to 350°F (180°C) and grease a 9 x 13–inch (23 x 33–cm) baking pan with coconut oil.

Drain the buckwheat and seeds through a sieve and transfer to a medium-sized bowl. Crack the eggs into the bowl and whisk into the soaked mixture along with the kefir. Then add the cinnamon, salt, nutmeg and fruit. Mix to combine all of the ingredients.

Pour into the prepared pan and bake for about 45 minutes, or until completely set. Remove from the oven and allow to cool for at least 5 minutes before serving. Drizzle with honey and serve with yogurt or fresh milk.

Frugal
Broth & Beans

Pots of two simple foods, broth and beans, have simmered over open fires and cast-iron cookstoves for generations. Beginning with bones and water, a pot of beans soon followed, simmered in that fragrant broth, seasoned with fresh onions, garlic and herbs. From that, the most frugal of soups were born.

But it doesn't stop there. These two staples are often consumed in our home every day, and often in combination. They help stretch expensive pastured proteins. A steaming bowl will warm and strengthen on cold days, whereas falafel and bean and potato patties top fresh salads at the height of scorching summers.

Yes, we eat beans nearly every day.

Besides the fact that the humble bean is very inexpensive, it also comes packed with fiber, protein, vitamins and minerals. When looking at longest-lived cultures, nearly all of them boast a daily consumption of black beans, lentils, kidney beans and many others native to their own land.

In combination with broth and small amounts of animal protein, beans are an excellent choice for the frugal table. But, you ask, how does one digest beans regularly? Well, there is evidence that your body's microbiome begins to adjust to the fibers and starches in beans over time, as long as you are feeding it good bacteria.

As a cook, however, there is a great deal we can do to mitigate against hard-to-digest beans. You must first make them digestible by unlocking the food potential from what is really a bean seed (see pages 42 and 143).

From a comforting bowl of soup (page 59), to a crispy falafel (page 47) or an easy-peasy baked supper (page 56), this chapter holds some of our most frugal of meals that we enjoy regularly. They will save you time and money, and leave you feeling nourished and satisfied.

How to Soak & Cook Beans for Better Digestion

Beans can be sprouted or soaked, depending on your preference for nutrition, time and flavor. Soaking beans for a long period of time, and changing the water frequently, is a common practice in most traditional cultures.

Sprouting or Soaking

Sprouting is one of the best ways to prepare beans for soaking. You can find a whole tutorial for it on page 143.

Sprouting takes a bit more time than soaking does and oftentimes, for certain recipes, I just use the soaking method. To soak beans and lentils, just cover them with plenty of water right in the pan you will be cooking them in.

Soak the beans for 12 to 48 hours. The longer, the better in terms of removing a lot of the "gassiness," which is really complex sugars. But for this to work well, you have to drain off the water about every 12 hours, more frequently when it's warm. If your kitchen is above 85°F (29°C), expect that those beans are going to start fermenting quickly. To prevent fermentation, pour off the water containing the fermentable starches present in the bean pot. Rinse and re-cover with fresh water.

Cooking

Once the beans have been fully soaked, it's time for cooking.

Pressure cooking is a great way to make beans more digestible. Some say it diminishes the lectins contained in beans, if that is a concern for you. You can use an old-fashioned pressure cooker, a modern electric pressure cooker or pressure can your beans. I have a recipe for the latter on the Nourishing Days blog. I don't know exactly why this is, but we do find that pressure canning beans results in an easier-to-digest bean. Also, if your beans are older and don't soften very well, pressure canning solves that problem, too.

To cook, cover again with about 2 inches (5 cm) of fresh water. Cook on the stovetop at a simmer or in the pressure cooker as directed by the manufacturer until the beans are completely tender.

What to Add & Avoid in Cooking

I find that beans will not go completely tender if acidity is involved in the cooking process. That means we don't add any citrus or tomatoes until the beans are completely tender. You can also mitigate the acidity of the beans themselves with a pinch of baking soda in the cooking water. This should help the skins come off a bit, which lends softness to the beans.

Certain herbs and spices have been found to help make beans more digestible. Add cumin, epazote or bay leaf to the pot for both flavor and digestion.

Soaked Grain-Free Garbanzo Bean Pizza Crust

Everyone needs a go-to pizza crust; this is ours. Combining high-protein garbanzo bean flour with the elasticity of tapioca starch makes for a chewy pizza crust that has just the right amount of crispness at the edges. Soaking the flours makes it easy to digest and gives the crust wonderful flavor. A nice light crust comes from the dual-leavening action of both yeast and baking powder. Don't be afraid to make a double batch and freeze the extra crust.

Makes
1 crust, 6 servings

1½ cups (180 g) garbanzo flour

1 cup (128 g) tapioca starch

1 cup (240 ml) water

1 tbsp (15 ml) apple cider vinegar

½ tsp instant yeast

Coconut oil, for lined baking sheet and hands

1 tbsp (14 g) baking powder

1½ tsp (9 g) salt

1 tbsp (4 g) ground psyllium husk

Cheese, meat, veggies and sauce, as desired, for topping

In a medium-sized bowl, whisk together the garbanzo flour and tapioca starch really well to combine. Pour in the water and vinegar and add the yeast. Whisk well, cover and let soak for 8 to 24 hours.

When ready to bake, preheat the oven to 450°F (230°C), line a baking sheet with parchment paper and oil it generously with coconut oil.

Uncover the dough and give it a quick stir before sprinkling with the baking powder, salt and psyllium. Mix everything together until completely combined. Let sit for 5 minutes to set up.

Using well-oiled hands, scoop the dough from the bowl and place it on the prepared baking sheet. Spread out the dough toward the edges of the pan, using your fingertips, oiling them as needed to keep the dough from sticking. Let the dough sit for 15 minutes to rise.

Place the dough in the oven and bake for 25 minutes, or until golden brown. Top with cheese, meat, veggies and sauce, as desired and return the pizza to the oven for 15 to 20 minutes, or until everything is warmed and melted.

Sprouted or Soaked Chickpea Falafel

Deeply golden and fried to crisp perfection, falafel were a hidden gem when I first discovered them. A classic Middle Eastern dish, we give it a twist by sprouting the beans and loading it up with tons of herbs and garlic. These hearty fried disks make excellent sandwich fillings, salad toppings or quick snacks. Best of all, the mixture refrigerates or freezes very well for quick meals anytime.

Serves

8

2 cups (400 g) dried chickpeas, sprouted (see page 143) or soaked in water for 24 to 48 hours

I large red onion, roughly chopped

I small bunch parsley

I small bunch cilantro

2 tsp (12 g) sea salt

I tsp red pepper flakes

8 cloves garlic

2½ tsp (6 g) ground cumin

2 tsp (9 g) baking powder

I to 2 tbsp (2 to 5 g) garbanzo bean flour

Lard, ghee or coconut oil, for frying

Wraps or bread plus a tangy sauce, such as Green Herb Sauce (page 98)

Drain and rinse the sprouted or soaked chickpeas and place in a food processor. Add the onion, parsley, cilantro, salt, red pepper flakes, garlic and cumin. Pulse until everything is roughly chopped and well combined, but be sure to stop before it begins to puree. It should be coarse like bread crumbs.

Scrape the mixture into a large bowl and sprinkle with the baking powder. Mix well. Test the consistency of the mixture by forming it into a walnut-sized ball in your hands. It should be tacky and moist, but should no longer stick to your hands. Add I to 2 tablespoons (2 to 5 g) of flour, at the most, if it is still too wet, keeping in mind that the rest period will help the mixture absorb more moisture.

Cover the bowl with a plate or plastic wrap and refrigerate for at least 2 to 3 hours before frying.

To fry: Place a 10-inch (25-cm) cast-iron skillet over medium heat and add enough of the lard to create a 1-inch (2.5-cm) depth of melted fat in the pan. Allow the lard to heat to approximately 375°F (190°C). You can test this by placing a tiny piece of the falafel mixture in the skillet and making sure it sizzles, or by using a thermometer.

Scoop up about 2 tablespoons (30 g) of the falafel mixture and loosely form an oval shape. Be careful not to compact the dough—you want that fluffy interior. Carefully place the mixture in the oil and repeat, filling the pan but leaving about ½ inch (1.3 cm) between mounds.

Continue to fry in batches until you have as many freshly fried falafel as you desire. Any remaining mixture can be refrigerated for up to 4 days or frozen.

Serve the falafel in a wrap, sandwich or atop bread with a tangy sauce, such as Green Herb Sauce.

Sweet Potato & Beet Soup

Thick and hearty, this soup is a combination of my two favorite root vegetables and a few strategically used spices. With its radiant color, this soup is a favorite, even among my pickiest soup eaters. And it couldn't be simpler to throw together.

Serves
4 to 6

¼ cup (55 g) ghee, lard or coconut oil

2 medium-sized onions, chopped

3 cloves garlic, minced

3 to 4 cups (710 to 950 ml) Bone Broth (page 150)

2 large beets, peeled and cut into ½" (1.3-cm) pieces

3 medium-sized sweet potatoes, peeled and cut into ½" (1.3-cm) pieces

2 tsp (12 g) sea salt, plus more as needed

2 tsp (5 g) ground cumin

1½ tsp (4 g) paprika

½ tsp red pepper flakes

1 (13.5-oz [400-ml]) can full-fat coconut milk or, if you prefer to use dairy, 1 cup (240 ml) raw whole milk + ½ cup (120 ml) raw heavy cream

2 tsp (10 ml) apple cider vinegar

⅓ cup (47 g) sunflower or pumpkin seeds, for garnish

Soaked Gluten-Free Artisan Bread (page 88), for serving

Place a Dutch oven over medium-high heat and add the ghee. Allow the ghee to melt and then add the onions. Cook, stirring occasionally, for 4 to 7 minutes, or until the onions just begin to caramelize. Add the garlic and cook an additional 2 minutes.

Add 3 cups (710 ml) of the broth plus the beets, sweet potatoes, salt, cumin, paprika and red pepper flakes. The broth should come just below the level of the vegetables, so add up to the additional cup (240 ml) of broth as needed. Bring to a simmer and then lower the heat to low. Simmer, partially covered, for 20 to 25 minutes, or until the vegetables are tender. Remove from the heat.

Transfer to a blender or use an immersion blender to blend the soup until smooth. Add the coconut milk and vinegar. Taste for salt and add more as needed.

Ladle into bowls and garnish with the sunflower or pumpkin seeds. Serve alongside the Soaked Gluten-Free Artisan Bread.

Kidney Bean–Potato Patties *(egg-free)*

Most bean burgers involve such ingredients as raw oats, bread crumbs and eggs. But I wanted something a little cleaner, simpler and cheaper. Beans and potatoes have got to be two of the most wholesome, filling and inexpensive foods out there, so they win the day. They come together in this recipe to form little patties that are crispy on the outside, creamy on the inside and a delicious burger substitute.

Serves
4

3 cups (768 g) cooked kidney beans, or 2 (14-oz [400-g]) cans, drained and rinsed

1 cup (175 g) potato flesh (from 1 to 2 boiled or baked potatoes; leftovers work great)

1 tsp salt

½ tsp garlic powder

½ tsp onion powder

Pinch of red pepper flakes

½ cup (56 g) masa flour

¼ cup (55 g) coconut oil, ghee or lard, for frying

Buns, rice or salad, plus salsa, hot sauce, avocado or your favorite toppings, for serving

In a medium-sized bowl, combine the beans and potato flesh. Using a potato masher, mash the kidney beans and potatoes until roughly mashed. Season with the salt, garlic powder, onion powder and red pepper flakes, and mix in the masa flour until a sticky dough forms. You should be able to form it into a ball, but it will still be tacky.

Place a 10-inch (25-cm) cast-iron or stainless-steel skillet over medium-high heat. Add ¼ cup (55 g) of the coconut oil to the pan and allow it to melt. Once hot, take approximately 3 tablespoons (45 g) of the bean mixture and form it into a thin patty no thicker than ¼ inch (6 mm).

Place 4 patties in the pan and allow to fry for 6 to 8 minutes, or until golden and crisp. Carefully flip and fry for an additional 6 to 8 minutes. Remove the patties from the pan once fully cooked and repeat with the remaining bean mixture.

Serve on buns, over rice or on top of a salad with salsa, hot sauce, avocado or your other favorite toppings.

Moroccan-Spiced Sprouted Chickpea Stew

In traditional food cultures around the globe, the legume is undeniably a staple food. Whether it is the black or pinto bean in South America or the chickpea of the Middle East, these cultures utilize these inexpensive staples on a daily basis. Such stews as this combine antioxidant-rich spices, the humble legume and traditional fats and broths into a frugal meal that can nourish a large crowd. The one thing that makes these legumes even better is a simple sprouting process you can do at home in just a few minutes per day.

Makes
6 to 8 servings

3 tbsp (42 g) lard or coconut oil

1 large onion, chopped

4 cloves garlic, minced

1 tbsp (7 g) ground cumin

1 tsp ground turmeric

½ tsp cayenne pepper

½ tsp ground cinnamon

½ tsp ground cardamom

½ tsp ground coriander

6 cups (1.4 L) chicken Bone Broth (page 150)

1 lb (455 g) dried chickpeas, sprouted (see page 143)

1 (28-oz [800-g]) can diced tomatoes

1 (12-oz [340-g]) can tomato sauce

Salt, to taste

Rice or sweet potatoes, grass-fed yogurt and minced cilantro, for serving

Place a Dutch oven over medium heat and melt the lard. Add the onion and sauté for about 5 minutes, or until translucent. Add the garlic, cumin, turmeric, cayenne, cinnamon, cardamom and coriander, and sauté for 2 minutes to bring out the aroma of the spices.

Add the chicken broth and scrape the bottom of the pot as the broth comes to a simmer. Add the sprouted chickpeas and bring to a boil. Lower the heat to a simmer and cook, uncovered, for 30 to 40 minutes, or until the chickpeas are tender.

Stir in the diced tomatoes and tomato sauce and continue to simmer for an additional 10 to 15 minutes, or until the sauce is nice and thick. Season generously with salt.

Serve over rice or baked sweet potatoes with a dollop of grass-fed yogurt and a sprinkle of minced cilantro.

Soaked Mexican Taco Pizza Bake

Yes, you can have your gluten-free pizza and eat it too! I like to pull out this dish—along with the other pizza recipe in this chapter—when we get into a food rut. A crispy bottom crust plays off of the creamy refried beans, spicy salsa and crunchy lettuce for a dynamic delight. You can find a super frugal homemade refried bean recipe on the Nourishing Days blog.

Serves
6

Crust

1¼ cups (207 g) sorghum flour

1½ cups (168 g) masa flour

2 cups (475 ml) water

2 tbsp (30 ml) apple cider vinegar

Coconut oil, for baking sheet

3 tbsp (45 ml) olive oil

2 tbsp (8 g) ground psyllium husk

1 tsp salt

2 tsp (9 g) baking powder

Toppings

2 cups (360 g) cooked beans, refried or regular

¾ cup (195 g) salsa

Olives, onions, bell peppers and cheese (optional), for topping

Crunchy lettuce, tomatoes, avocado or sour cream, for serving

In a medium-sized bowl, stir together the sorghum flour, masa flour, water and vinegar. Once the flours are well hydrated, cover and allow to soak for 8 to 24 hours.

Preheat the oven to 450°F (230°C). Line a large baking sheet with parchment and oil the parchment generously with coconut oil.

To the soaked flour mixture, add the olive oil, psyllium, salt and baking powder. Mix well and let sit for 5 minutes to hydrate. Using wet hands, spread out the dough to the edges of the pan, leaving a tiny lip of dough at the outer edges. Poke all over with a fork. Bake for 25 to 35 minutes, or until golden brown all over.

Spread the beans evenly over the baked crust. Spoon the salsa over the refried beans and top with whatever toppings you choose. Return the pizza to the oven to bake for an additional 10 minutes to warm all the ingredients or melt the cheese, as needed.

Serve topped with lettuce, tomatoes, avocado or sour cream.

Versatile Oven-Baked Rice & Lentils

This one-pan wonder was born just after the birth of our third child. Something you can throw together between caring for little ones or working on deadlines, this dish has become a regular staple in our home. It might not seem all that exciting, that classic combination of rice and lentils, but it works well with a bit of onion and seasoning and pairs great with a jar of kraut for a meal so simple you can make it with a newborn in your arms and a toddler at your feet.

Serves
6

¼ cup (55 g) coconut oil

1½ cups (300 g) lentils, sprouted (see page 143)

2 cups (390 g) uncooked jasmine rice

1 onion, peeled and diced

5½ cups (1.3 L) Bone Broth (page 150) or water

2 tsp (5 g) chili powder

2 tsp (12 g) salt

Salad, vegetable ferments, plus cheese, avocado or salsa, for serving

Preheat the oven to 375°F (190°C). Place the coconut oil in a 9 x 13–inch (23 x 33–cm) baking pan and melt in the oven as it preheats.

Once the coconut oil is melted, add the lentils, rice and onion to the pan. Add the broth and seasonings and mix with a fork until all the ingredients are evenly distributed. Cover with a tight-fitting lid or aluminum foil. Bake for 60 to 70 minutes, or until all the liquid absorbs and the lentils and rice are tender.

Serve with a salad, vegetable ferments and cheese, avocado, salsa or other toppings.

Note: The flavor options for this recipe are endless. For a curried version, replace the chili powder with a tablespoon (6 g) of your favorite curry powder and replace 1½ cups (355 ml) of the broth with equal amounts of coconut milk. Or, for an Italian twist, replace the chili powder with an equal quantity of Italian seasoning, 2 teaspoons (6 g) of garlic powder and a pinch of red pepper flakes.

Family Favorite "White" Soup

Despite the simplest of frugal ingredients, this soup is one of those rare better-than-the-sum-of-its-parts dishes. Even the pickiest of our children love it even when they turn their nose up at plenty of other soups. It cooks up thick and creamy with a flavor that reminds me of the gravy you get at that infamous fried chicken restaurant. Perfectly comforting and nourishing on cold days.

Serves
8 to 10

¼ cup (55 g) lard, coconut oil or ghee

1 onion, diced

1 medium-sized cabbage (2 to 2.5 lb [905 g to 1.1 kg]), sliced thinly

6 cups (1 kg) cooked navy beans

1 cup (195 g) sprouted brown or white rice

8 cups (1.9 L) Bone Broth (page 150)

1 tbsp (4 g) minced fresh parsley

½ tsp freshly ground black pepper, plus more as needed

1 tbsp (18 g) sea salt, plus more as needed

In a large Dutch oven over medium-high heat, melt the lard and add the onion. Sauté for 3 to 5 minutes, or until the onion is translucent. Add the cabbage, beans, rice, broth, parsley, pepper and salt, and bring to a simmer.

Lower the heat to low and cook, partially covered, for 25 to 30 minutes, or until the cabbage and rice are both cooked through. If you'd like the soup to be a little thicker, cook, uncovered, for an additional 5 minutes.

Taste the soup and add more salt and pepper, as needed. Serve hot.

Real Food Copycat Tomato Soup

Who else was a child of the '80s and ate grilled cheese dipped into Campbell's tomato soup? Creamy, tangy, with just a hint of sweetness, that soup brings back memories. This recipe is spot-on what I remember from my youth and one of the least expensive meals we make.

Serves
8

2 qt (1.9 L) Bone Broth (page 150)

3 (6-oz [170-g]) cans tomato paste

2¼ tsp (scant 14 g) salt

¾ tsp onion powder

¾ tsp garlic powder

¼ tsp freshly ground black pepper, plus more for serving (optional)

1 tbsp (15 ml) apple cider vinegar

3 tbsp (60 g) honey, preferably raw

½ cup (120 ml) coconut milk or raw heavy cream, plus more for serving

Fresh basil, for serving (optional)

In a medium-sized saucepan, bring the broth to a simmer over medium heat. Whisk in the tomato paste until smooth. Lower the heat to medium-low, and season with the salt, onion powder, garlic powder, pepper, vinegar and honey. Taste and adjust the seasonings according to your taste.

Stir in the coconut milk and serve, garnished with additional coconut milk, fresh basil or pepper.

Economical Pastured Proteins

A big steak is among my favorite meals; in that, I am sure I am not alone. But it's something that I only eat on occasion . . . maybe once or twice a year, actually. I am not alone in my carnivorous ways. Our whole family enjoys eating all manner of meats from chicken to beef roast, goat to bacon, sausage to a fresh fish fillet.

But we don't eat a lot of it, at least not as much as we could. On our homestead, we have started to produce some of our own meat over the last few years. This includes a couple of runs of meat birds a year, a beef steer every year or two and most recently, pork.

Harvest times are a sobering reminder of what it takes to put meat on the table: the daily care of the animals, the choosing of higher-quality feeds when it costs a bit more and ultimately the taking of a life when we harvest our own meat. Knowing all that goes into a simple chicken dinner is also why we are willing to pay a little more for higher-quality meat when we need to buy it.

When we harvest chickens, we enjoy chicken dinners regularly. When we harvest beef, steaks and hamburgers make the menu when they normally would not. We really enjoy these times, but they only last a few short weeks and we pressure can the rest, or put away a bit in our solar freezer.

(Continued)

The rest of the year, we stretch out meat as far as we can. Rarely does meat make the centerpiece of the meal. Instead, it stands as an accompaniment to vegetables, plenty of healthy fats and simple starches for those who can eat them. That's partially because we are a family of eight and partially because I am personally convinced that while meat that has been raised properly is both ethical to eat and nourishing to our bodies, we could stand to eat a little less animal flesh and a little more of the other animal products, such as bone broth, fats, offal, eggs and the like.

When we are in a season of needing to buy our meat, we usually stick to four options that we have chosen both for frugality and their nutrient density. In the order of the frequency that we tend to eat them, these four are:

- Grass-fed ground beef
- Canned wild Alaskan salmon
- Pasture-raised whole chickens
- Offal

Yes, offal. We don't eat it often, due to its scarcity in the area we live, but liver and heart are two that we've learned to eat and actually enjoy when cooked up in the recipes I share in this chapter. The other recipes in this chapter utilize beef, salmon and chicken more as an accompaniment to other foods than the main event. But trust me, your wallet will be the only one who knows you are stretching the meat.

Dutch Oven Whole Roasted Chicken Cacciatore with Brown Rice

Besides a simple roast chicken, this is one of our favorite ways to eat a whole chicken. It also happens to be a dead-simple, one-pan meal that includes veggies and rice right in the chicken pan. The rice absorbs all of the chicken juices and herbs, and makes a great base for the chicken, peppers and onions. The tricky part of this recipe is that chickens have varying moisture levels. Grocery store chickens are usually injected with a water solution that messes with the water needed for the rice to cook. The broth/water volume in this recipe is based on the use of a pasture-raised chicken.

Serves
6 to 8

¹/₃ cup (75 g) coconut oil or lard

3 cups (585 g) brown rice, soaked or sprouted (see page 143)

I (4- to 5-lb [1.8- to 2.3-kg]) chicken

2 tsp (12 g) salt (omit if using a salted broth) to season vegetables and rice, plus more for seasoning chicken

Freshly ground black pepper, for seasoning chicken

2 large yellow onions, sliced

3 bell peppers, seeded and sliced

I (24-oz [680-g]) can diced tomatoes

I (15-oz [425-g]) can tomato sauce

1½ tsp (2 g) dried oregano

1½ tsp (1 g) dried basil

2 tsp (4 g) garlic powder

½ to I tsp red pepper flakes, depending on how much heat you like

5 cups (1.2 L) Bone Broth (page 150) or water

Preheat the oven to 450°F (230°C).

Add the oil to a large, oval roasting pan with a lid and move it around to generously coat the bottom and halfway up the sides. To the oiled pan, add the soaked brown rice. Stir it around in the pan to coat the grains of rice in the oil and then push the rice to the sides to create a space for the chicken.

Season the chicken generously with salt and black pepper. Place the chicken, breast side up, in the middle of the pan in the middle of the rice. Place the sliced onions and bell peppers on top of the rice and the chicken. Pour the diced tomatoes and tomato sauce over the rice, distributing them evenly as you go. Sprinkle the oregano, basil, garlic powder and red pepper flakes over the chicken, rice and vegetables and then pour the broth over the vegetables and rice. Sprinkle the salt over the vegetables and rice. Bake, covered, for I hour.

Remove the pan from the oven and remove the lid. Use a fork to stir the rice and vegetables to see how they are cooking. If there is little liquid left in the pan and the rice is still undercooked, add up to an additional ½ cup (120 ml) of liquid to the pan and place back in the oven. If there is still plenty of moisture, or if the rice is mostly cooked, place the pan back into the oven, uncovered, for an additional 45 minutes. This will help the chicken finish cooking and brown the skin slightly.

(Continued)

Dutch Oven Whole Roasted Chicken Cacciatore with Brown Rice *(Continued)*

After 30 minutes, check to see that the rice and chicken are both cooked through. The rice should be tender and the chicken should be cooked to an internal temperature of 180°F (82°C). If not, place back in the oven for an additional 10 to 15 minutes.

Once fully cooked, transfer the chicken to a cutting board or platter and let rest for 15 minutes before slicing. Meanwhile, fluff the rice with a fork while simultaneously mixing in the vegetables. Taste and add salt, as needed. Once the chicken has rested, cut off the legs, thighs and breast meat and serve over the rice and vegetable mixture.

Set aside the chicken carcass—and save the bones after serving—for homemade bone broth (page 150).

When You Just Can't Afford Good Meat

Sometimes we have to make tough decisions when things get tight. Meat being as expensive as it is, it is often one of the first purchases we re-consider. There are varying theories on what to do if you can't afford pasture-raised meat. One theory is to cut out meat and become a vegetarian. Another is to eat less meat so that you can afford higher quality. Yet another is to just buy conventional meat and not sweat it.

My personal approach is to combine all three. At times when we can't afford the highest-quality meats, I consider a few things: First, how can we cut back so that we don't have to buy conventional meat? Second, if necessary, what is our second-best option? From a sustainability and care for the animals standpoint, not eating meat (or eating far less of it) is probably the best option. From a health standpoint, if you feel you *need* meat, buying lean cuts and adding healthy fats, such as coconut oil, is your best bet. At various times, I have used this approach because fat concentrates the contaminants that result from factory farming (i.e., estrogen disruptors, inflammatory fatty acids, chemical residues, etc.). That's not to say that the meat itself doesn't also contain contaminants; it just isn't quite as concentrated.

With that said, I really prefer to lower our meat consumption, up our healthy fats (or carbs for those who need more) and buy or raise higher-quality animal products.

Master Stir-Fry

If you're not eating stir-fry at least once a week, you are missing out. Why? Because you can use whatever vegetables and protein you have, it really stretches the meat when served over rice and it is packed with fresh vegetables and flavor. If you desire to eat seasonal produce, this dish will change every few months to contain the freshest of ingredients. So, put on a pot of rice and by the time it's through cooking, this stir-fry will hit the table.

Serves

6 to 8

¼ cup (55 g) lard, coconut oil or ghee

2 medium-sized onions, sliced

½ to 1 lb (225 to 455 g) ground grass-fed beef or raw chicken pieces

1 lb (455 g) Brassicas (broccoli, cabbage, cauliflower, etc., mixed or a single kind), chopped

1 large bunch kale or collards, chopped finely

2 cups (about 250 g) chopped other vegetables (bell peppers, zucchini, carrots, celery, mushrooms, etc.)

Salt

1 tbsp (15 ml) apple cider vinegar

2 tbsp (40 g) raw honey

4 cloves garlic, minced

½ tsp ground ginger

1 tsp red pepper flakes

2 cups (475 ml) Bone Broth (page 150)

1½ tbsp (12 g) tapioca starch

Rice or salad, for serving

In a wok or large skillet, heat the lard over high heat. Add the onions and cook, stirring frequently, for 3 to 5 minutes, or until they just start to turn golden. Add the meat and stir-fry until it just starts to brown. Add the Brassicas, greens and other vegetables and season everything with salt. Continue to cook for an additional 5 minutes.

While the vegetables finish cooking, make the sauce: In a pint-sized (500-ml) jar, combine the vinegar, honey, garlic, ginger, red pepper flakes, broth and tapioca starch. Put a lid on the jar and shake vigorously. Remove the lid and stir the sauce with a fork to make sure that the tapioca starch is dissolved completely.

Once the vegetables are just about cooked through, slowly add the sauce, stirring constantly to evenly distribute it. Cook for an additional 2 to 4 minutes, allowing the sauce to thicken and coat everything.

Serve over rice or alongside a fresh salad.

Kenyan Pilau

Reminiscent of what we refer to in the United States as dirty rice, this one-pan meal of rice, vegetables and meat is on frequent rotation in our home. Everything cooks up fragrant with spices and aromatics in one pot and it can be served easily with a side salad, vegetable or kraut. Don't let the longer list of ingredients fool you; this is one of the simplest meals to put together.

Serves
6 to 8

¼ cup (55 g) coconut oil, ghee or lard

I large onion, diced

I bell pepper, diced

2 medium-sized carrots, diced

I medium-sized zucchini, diced

I lb (455 g) grass-fed ground beef

3 cloves garlic, minced

I tbsp (6 g) minced fresh ginger, or I tsp dried

I tsp freshly ground black pepper

2 tsp (5 g) ground cumin

Pinch of ground cinnamon

I tbsp (18 g) salt

½ tsp red pepper flakes (omit if your family doesn't like spicy food)

2 cups (390 g) uncooked jasmine rice

4 cups (946 ml) Bone Broth (page 150) or water

I (6-oz [170-g]) can tomato paste

I bunch cilantro, finely chopped

Salad or fermented vegetables, for serving

In a Dutch oven, heat the coconut oil over medium-high heat. Add the onion, bell pepper, carrots and zucchini and sauté, stirring occasionally, for 8 to 10 minutes, or until the vegetables start to soften. Add the beef and cook with the vegetables for 5 to 10 minutes, or until it starts to brown. Add the garlic, ginger, black pepper, cumin, cinnamon, salt and red pepper flakes and cook, stirring, for I minute.

Pour in the rice and stir. Allow to cook about 3 minutes to toast the rice. Add the broth and tomato paste and stir well to dissolve the paste. Bring to a boil, add the chopped cilantro and lower the heat to low. Simmer for 15 to 20 minutes, or until the rice has absorbed all of the liquid.

Remove from the heat and let rest, covered, for 10 minutes before gently stirring and serving. Serve with a salad or fermented vegetables on the side.

Creamy Dairy-Free Salmon-Stuffed Potatoes

I am forever trying to work the humble potato into the main part of our meal. They are inexpensive and a very wholesome source of starch for a growing family. Combine them with frugal canned salmon and avocado and you've got a main dish as satisfying as it is penny-pinching. These are great warm, but also work really well as a picnic item at room temperature. And, if you have someone in your brood who can't eat potatoes, just set aside their salmon-avocado mixture and serve it with some raw veggies.

Serves
6

6 large or 12 smaller baking potatoes (3 to 4 lb [1.4 to 1.8 kg])

2 tbsp (28 g) coconut oil, lard or ghee

½ large onion, minced

Juice of 1 large lemon

2 small avocados, pitted

1 (14.5-oz [411-g]) can wild Alaskan salmon, drained

½ tsp freshly ground black pepper

Salt

Preheat the oven to 400°F (200°C).

Place the potatoes in a 9 x 13–inch (23 x 33–cm) glass baking pan. Oil the potatoes all over with the coconut oil. Bake for 45 to 60 minutes, or until tender. Remove from the oven and let rest at least 15 minutes, or until you can handle them.

Cut off the top of each potato, scoop out the flesh and transfer to a medium-sized bowl, reserving the skins. Add the onion, lemon juice and avocado flesh to the potatoes and mash thoroughly with a potato masher.

Add the drained salmon, black pepper and a generous sprinkle of salt. Stir to combine. Taste and adjust the salt as needed.

Stuff the potato skins with the mixture. Place back in the oven to warm for 10 minutes or serve directly.

Mediterranean Hide-the-Heart Meatballs

Beef heart is one of those foods that nobody wants to talk about. It's not glamorous, but it is really, really good for you. And it doesn't have that really awful offal taste that so many complain of. When it's hidden with some ground beef and spiked with loads of fresh herbs, citrus and garlic, you barely even know it's there. If you know your local farmer or butcher, you can even ask that the ground beef and heart be mixed for you at your desired ratio for this dish.

Serves
4 to 6

1 medium-sized onion, finely chopped

6 cloves garlic, finely minced

1 bunch fresh parsley, finely minced

½ bunch cilantro, finely minced

2 tbsp (8 g) ground psyllium husk or (14 g) coconut flour

2 tsp (12 g) sea salt

½ tsp freshly ground black pepper

¼ tsp red pepper flakes

Juice of 1 large lemon

1 lb (455 g) grass-fed ground beef

8 oz (225 g) grass-fed ground beef heart

Coconut oil, lard or ghee, for frying

Green Herb Sauce (page 98) or tzatziki sauce, plus rice or salad, for serving

Heat a skillet over medium heat.

Meanwhile, in a medium-sized bowl, combine the onion, garlic, parsley, cilantro, psyllium, salt, black pepper, red pepper flakes and lemon juice, and whisk together with a fork. Transfer the ground beef and heart to the bowl and, with your fingertips, gently work everything together. Avoid compacting the mixture between your fingers, so you keep the mixture light.

Place 2 tablespoons (28 g) of the coconut oil in the skillet and allow it to melt. Form small meatballs, about 1 inch (2.5 cm) in diameter, and place carefully in the hot skillet, allowing ¼ inch (6 mm) between meatballs and working in batches so as to not crowd the pan. Allow to cook for 4 to 5 minutes, or until deeply golden brown. Carefully turn the meatballs to brown the other side and cook for an additional 4 to 5 minutes, or until cooked through. Transfer to a plate and finish frying the remaining meat mixture.

To serve, drizzle with Green Herb Sauce or a tzatziki sauce, and serve alongside rice or atop a salad.

Chicken Livers and Gravy *(that we actually like)*

Of all the organ meats, liver is the most ubiquitous. It is also something most of us serve for health reasons and not flavor. But there are some tricks to cooking liver in a way that makes the best of it. And this particular recipe is my favorite way to serve chicken livers, the livers sort of disappearing into a mushroom gravy. If you're struggling with getting your family to eat liver, I'd give this one a try.

Serves
4

1 lb (455 g) chicken livers

Juice of ½ lemon

4 strips bacon, diced

Coconut oil, lard or ghee, for frying

1 (10-oz [280-g]) package mushrooms, sliced

2 medium-sized yellow onions, sliced

2 cups (475 ml) Bone Broth (page 150), divided

4 tsp (11 g) arrowroot or (12 g) potato starch

¼ tsp freshly ground black pepper

Salt

Mashed potatoes, rice or vegetables, for serving

Rinse the chicken livers well. Cut them into ¼-inch (6-mm) pieces and place in a bowl. Cover with water, add the lemon juice and refrigerate for 1 hour. When ready to cook, drain and pat dry.

Place a large skillet over medium heat and add the bacon. Cook, stirring occasionally, until the bacon is crisp and the fat has rendered. Transfer the bacon to a platter. Increase the heat to medium-high and allow the bacon fat to get very hot.

Add half of the drained liver pieces to the hot skillet and cook, undisturbed, for 2 minutes. Turn and cook the other side for 2 more minutes. Transfer to the platter of bacon and repeat with the second half of the livers.

Add a couple of tablespoons (14 to 28 g) of coconut oil to the pan, if needed, and add the mushrooms to the pan. Cook, undisturbed, for 4 minutes, then stir and cook until they are completely caramelized and cooked, about 4 minutes. Transfer to the platter and repeat with the onions, adding a couple more tablespoons of coconut oil, as needed.

Once the pan is empty, add 1½ cups (355 ml) of the broth to the pan. Bring to a simmer. While that heats up, in a small bowl, mix the remaining ½ cup (120 ml) of broth with the starch and stir with a fork to make a slurry. Once the broth is simmering, slowly pour in the slurry while stirring constantly. Scrape the bottom of the pan as you go, to get up any caramelized bits from the pan, and season with the pepper and plenty of salt. Cook and whisk the gravy until thickened.

Add the liver, bacon, mushrooms and onions back to the pan and cook for 1 to 2 minutes, or until everything is just heated through. Remove from the heat and serve over mashed potatoes, rice or vegetables.

Tamale Pie

The original version of this recipe, filled with plenty of meat, is more of a treat meal for us than most of the recipes in this book. It makes a great main dish for a potluck. For our everyday meals, however, we cut back the chicken to 1 cup (160 g) and add 2 cups (354 g) of prepared beans.

Serves
8

2 cups (224 g) organic masa flour

1½ tsp (7 g) baking powder

½ tsp salt, plus more to taste

½ cup (112 g) cold lard or unsalted butter, cut into pieces

2 cups + 1½ cups (830 ml) Bone Broth (page 150), divided

¼ cup (55 g) coconut oil or lard, plus more for baking dish

2 large onions, chopped

¼ to ½ tsp cayenne pepper, plus more to taste

1 tbsp (7 g) paprika

2 tsp (2 g) dried oregano

3 cloves garlic, minced

1 tsp ground cumin

3 cups (480 g) cooked and shredded chicken or 1 cup (160 g) chicken + 2 cups (354 g) prepared beans

1 (6-oz [170-g]) can tomato paste

1 tbsp (15 ml) apple cider vinegar

Lettuce, tomato, onion, avocado, sour cream, salsa or your favorite taco toppings, to serve

Spanish Quinoa (page 101), to serve

For the topping, in a small bowl, mix together the masa, baking powder and salt. Cut in the lard by using two forks or a pastry cutter to cut (and mix) the lard into pea-sized pieces. Add 2 cups (475 ml) of the broth and mix until a wet dough is formed. Set aside.

For the filling, in a large saucepan over high heat, melt the coconut oil. Add the onions and sauté, stirring occasionally, for 5 to 7 minutes, or until translucent. Add the cayenne, paprika, oregano, garlic and cumin and sauté for 2 more minutes, stirring constantly.

Add the remaining broth, cooked chicken (plus beans or vegetables, if using), tomato paste and vinegar and season generously with salt. Simmer over low heat for 30 minutes.

Meanwhile, preheat the oven to 400°F (200°C) and grease a 9 x 13–inch (23 x 33–cm) baking dish with coconut oil.

Once the filling is done cooking, taste it for seasoning. Add more salt and cayenne as desired and transfer the mixture to the prepared baking dish. Smooth out the filling, using a fork, then spoon the masa topping over it, spreading out the masa mixture evenly—don't worry about the filling peeking through or the masa topping looking rustic.

Place the baking dish atop a sheet pan to prevent any of the bubbling mixture from spilling out onto the oven. Transfer the pan to the oven. Bake for 45 to 55 minutes, or until the topping is golden and cooked through.

Remove from the oven and allow to cool for at least 30 minutes before serving. Serve topped with lettuce, tomato, onion, avocado, sour cream, salsa or your favorite taco toppings and Spanish Quinoa.

Crispy Oven-Baked Salmon Burgers

Salmon burgers are one of our favorite main dishes and absolutely delicious with their browned, crisped edges. But standing over a skillet with a baby on your hip and a toddler at your feet isn't always doable. So, I figured out a way to throw these salmon patties in the oven and walk away, knowing they will still come out golden and crisp.

Makes
24 salmon patties

½ cup (112 g) coconut oil, ghee or lard

2 large, pasture-raised eggs

½ medium-sized onion, minced

2 cloves garlic, minced

1 tsp sea salt

2 tbsp (30 ml) fresh lemon juice

⅛ tsp cayenne

2 (14.5-oz [411-g]) cans wild Alaskan salmon, drained

3 tbsp (21 g) coconut flour

Preheat the oven to 450°F (230°C). Drizzle ¾ teaspoon of the coconut oil into each well of two 12-well muffin pans.

In a medium-sized bowl, whisk the eggs. Add the onion and garlic and whisk together. Add the salt, lemon juice, cayenne and drained salmon. Mix everything well with a fork. Sprinkle with the coconut flour and mix everything together until homogenous.

Divide the salmon mixture into 24 equal segments, using a spatula or your hands. Compact each portion of salmon mixture into a patty and press it evenly into one of the prepared muffin wells. Repeat with the remaining mixture and muffin wells.

Brush the remaining coconut oil over each portion of salmon. Bake for 35 to 45 minutes, or until crispy and golden around the edges.

Remove from the oven and allow to cool for about 5 minutes before carefully removing and serving.

Serve on gluten-free bread (page 88) or alongside vegetables and rice.

Stretch-the-Meat and Bean Loaf

Meat loaf is, of course, a classic family favorite. But to make enough for our family would require 2 to 3 pounds (905 g to 1.4 kg) of meat. So, I throw some beans and vegetables in the mixture for a barbecue-inspired meat loaf with half the meat.

Serves

6 to 8

2 tbsp (28 g) coconut oil, for pan

2 large, pasture-raised eggs

2 cups (512 g) prepared kidney or black beans (see page 143)

1 onion, diced

1 zucchini, diced (about 1¼ cups [150 g])

2 tbsp (40 g) raw honey

1 (6-oz [170-g]) can tomato paste

½ tsp red pepper flakes

½ tsp ground cumin

2 tsp (12 g) salt

1 tsp paprika

1 lb (455 g) ground beef

1 cup (112 g) masa flour

Preheat the oven to 350°F (180°C). Lightly grease a 9 x 5–inch (23 x 12.5–cm) glass loaf pan with the coconut oil.

In a medium-sized bowl, whisk the eggs and then add the beans. Use a fork to mash the beans roughly into the eggs. Then stir in the onion, zucchini, honey, tomato paste, red pepper flakes, cumin, salt and paprika. Stir everything together well with a fork.

Add the beef and gently mix it in with your fingertips—do not squish it together with your hands. Sprinkle the masa flour over the mixture and stir until everything seems well incorporated.

Transfer the meat mixture to the prepared loaf pan and bake for 45 to 60 minutes, or until the meat is cooked to a temperature of 180°F (82°C).

Remove from the oven and allow to cool for 10 minutes before slicing and serving.

Salmon Salad *(mayo-free)*

For many of us, tuna salad tastes of our youth. Spread between slices of white bread and tucked into lunch boxes, it was the mayo-filled days before we learned what was in that mayo. Now, as adults, we often crave those flavors but without all the processed soy oil. This salad fills that void and is excellent spread between slices of the Soaked Gluten-Free Artisan Bread (page 88).

Serves
6

3 very ripe avocados, pitted

½ large red onion, diced

Juice of 1 lemon

3 ribs celery, diced

2 (14.5-oz [411-g]) cans wild Alaskan salmon, drained

Salt and freshly ground black pepper

Scoop the avocado flesh into a medium-sized bowl. Mash it well with a fork and add the onion, lemon juice and celery. Add the salmon and combine everything well with a fork. Add salt and pepper, to taste.

Serve inside sandwiches or atop a green salad.

Spiced Thai Coconut Chicken

This is one of my favorite things to make with leftover roasted chicken—and it's fast, too! Just put on a pot of rice (or a pan of Szechuan Vegetables [page 102]), cook up a quick sauce and add the chicken. In 20 minutes, a rich, flavorful dinner is ready. Thai basil is a little hard to find, so feel free to substitute cilantro for a flavor twist.

Serves

4

1 (13.5-oz [400-ml]) can full-fat coconut milk, or 1½ cups (355 ml) homemade (page 136)

1 cup (240 ml) Bone Broth (page 150)

½ tsp cayenne pepper

4 cloves garlic, minced

½ tsp ground ginger

1½ tsp (3 g) ground turmeric

1 tsp apple cider vinegar

2 tbsp (40 g) honey, preferably raw

2½ cups (350 g) leftover roasted chicken

½ cup lightly packed (20 g) Thai basil leaves, chopped

Salt

Rice, steamed vegetables or Szechuan Vegetables (page 102)

In a 12-inch (35-cm) skillet, combine the coconut milk, broth, cayenne, garlic, ginger, turmeric, vinegar and honey and place over medium-high heat. Bring to a low simmer. Add the chicken and simmer for 5 minutes to thicken the sauce and meld the flavors.

Remove from the heat and stir in the Thai basil. Add salt, to taste.

Serve over cooked rice, steamed vegetables or Szechuan Vegetables.

Sensible Accompaniments

It is not uncommon for our meals to consist of a one-pot main dish from the previous two chapters along with a simple jar (or jars) of fermented vegetables or a simple salad. That is nourishing food in its most simple—and often best—form. But some meals are more a mélange of a little vegetables, a little starch and a little protein, all garnished with healthy fats. And oftentimes, they are a few of the dishes you'll see in this chapter.

Plant foods are amazing, yet sometimes underrated by the traditional foods community, and I really like to make them a good part of a lot of our meals. But mostly, we eat them very simply: just steamed or stir-fried, as raw salad with oil and vinegar and as pots of good ol' collard or kale greens.

But I know you don't need a recipe for those foods. Instead, what I've included in this chapter are some of our favorite unique ways to eat vegetables, those starchy sides so many love and a few snacky dips and sauces we eat often.

My favorite recipe of this chapter, however, is one I've been working on for well over a year. When you are gluten-free, bread is obviously something you might miss. And to purchase good gluten-free bread can cost you upward of $5 to $8 per small loaf. No thanks.

To fill that void, I developed a recipe for a gluten-free bread that honestly is almost indiscernible from an artisan wheat loaf. And, to make it more digestible, it is soaked or soured overnight.

This chapter is a testament to the fact that one of the best ways to work around eating really simple, frugal food is to serve a variety: a hummus or guacamole dip, a loaf of bread and a salad or a pan of stir-fried vegetables, a pot of rice and a shake from the treats chapter. And, of course, putting out a sheet pan of crispy hash browns with some fruit and fried greens and eggs as breakfast for dinner will win the day every time.

So, use a little of this and a little of that and create a table that feels like abundance without ever breaking the bank.

Soaked Gluten-Free Artisan Bread

It has taken me a lot of trial and error to get to this point, but I am happy to say this bread is nearly indistinguishable from the crunchy-crusted, chewy-centered wheat breads we lovingly call artisan. The flour combination is light and the high hydration really gives it a nice rise with a lovely open crumb. Best of all, it is a supersimple dough that can be soaked for days for optimal digestion.

Makes

1 large loaf

2¼ cups (535 ml) water

2 tbsp (30 ml) apple cider vinegar

1 tbsp (18 g) salt

3 tbsp (60 g) honey

2 tbsp (8 g) ground psyllium husk

1¼ cups (172 g) sorghum flour

¾ cup (96 g) tapioca starch

¾ cup (114 g) potato starch

¾ cup (90 g) garbanzo flour

½ tsp instant yeast

Coconut or olive oil, for pan and hands

In a large bowl, whisk together the water, vinegar, salt and honey. Sprinkle with the psyllium and immediately whisk for a couple of minutes, or until it begins to gel. Let the mixture sit for 2 to 3 minutes, or until the psyllium has fully gelled.

Meanwhile, in a separate bowl, combine the sorghum flour, tapioca starch, potato starch, garbanzo flour and instant yeast and whisk together really well. Add this dry mixture to the psyllium mixture and mix well, using a wooden spoon, until a sticky, shaggy dough comes together. You can switch over to mixing with your hands to better combine all of the ingredients.

Cover the bowl and leave the dough to sit for 12 to 18 hours at room temperature. If you'd like to soak the dough for even longer, you can place it in the refrigerator after 12 hours and chill it for up to 48 hours. During this time, the dough will increase in volume.

When you are ready to bake the bread, preheat your oven to 425°F (220°C) and grease a baking sheet with oil.

Punch down the dough. Divide the dough into 2 small loaves or a dozen rolls. Using greased hands, shape each of these into a tall round and then transfer them to the prepared baking sheet.

Cover the bread with plastic wrap or a damp towel and leave to rise for 30 minutes or, if you are making rolls, rise for 20 minutes.

Bake the bread for 50 to 60 minutes, or the rolls for 30 to 40 minutes, or until golden brown.

Whole-Olive Hummus

A staple in some Middle Eastern cuisines, hummus is a wonderfully creamy dip or spread for snacking or as a part of a meal. Instead of drizzling in a bunch of olive oil, I find whole olives give a great flavor and are also a more frugal addition. If you love garlic as much as we do, go with the full eight cloves. And if, like us, you like tahini as much as we do in our hummus, buy it in bulk for a great deal of savings.

Serves

8

2 cups (400 g) dried chickpeas

Generous pinch of baking soda

½ cup (120 g) tahini

1 (6-oz [170-g]) can or jar green olives

6 to 8 cloves garlic

1 tbsp (7 g) ground cumin

Juice of 2 large lemons, plus more to taste

2 tsp (12 g) salt, plus more to taste

Water, as needed, to thin

Sprout the chickpeas according to the tutorial on page 143 and place in a medium-sized pot. Alternatively, if you just want soaked chickpeas, place them in a medium-sized pot and cover with 6 cups (1.4 L) of water. Allow to soak for 24 to 48 hours, draining and rinsing every 12 hours to prevent fermentation.

Once the chickpeas are sprouted or soaked, cover them with 2 inches (5 cm) of fresh water and place the pot over high heat. Add the baking soda and bring to a boil. Lower the heat to a simmer and allow to cook, partially covered, for 30 to 40 minutes, or until the chickpeas are completely tender.

Drain the chickpeas and transfer them to a food processor, blender or a clean bowl if using an immersion blender. Add the tahini, olives, garlic, cumin, lemon juice and salt, and blend until completely smooth, stopping to scrape down the sides of the food processor, adding water as needed to thin it out. Taste and add additional salt and lemon juice, as desired.

Stretched-Out Guacamole

Guacamole is a great way to add in some extra healthy fats to a meal. Creamy, rich and full of flavor, this Mexican-inspired recipe is a hit as either a dip or topping. The one downside is that avocados can be very pricey, depending on where you live. To combat that, I like to use the humble bean to stretch the creamy avocado. It also adds protein and fiber and really bulks the dish up for a crowd. What it doesn't do is compromise on flavor.

Serves
8

3 cups (768 g) cooked chickpeas (see page 143)

4 medium-sized avocados, peeled and pitted

1 medium-sized red onion, diced

¼ cup (60 ml) freshly squeezed lemon juice

½ cup (20 g) chopped fresh cilantro

½ cup (90 g) diced tomato

3 cloves garlic, minced

1½ tsp (9 g) sea salt, plus more as needed

2 jalapeño peppers, seeded and diced (optional)

Veggies, chips, tacos, beans or bread, for serving

In a medium-sized bowl, mash the chickpeas roughly, using a potato masher. When they are very chunky, add the avocado flesh and continue to mash until mostly smooth.

Using a fork, mix in the onion, lemon juice, cilantro, tomato, garlic, salt and jalapeños, if using. Taste and adjust the salt, as needed.

Serve with veggies, chips, tacos, beans, or as a sandwich filling.

Sheet Pan Hash Browns

Not just for breakfast, these delicious oven-crisped hash browns are great at any meal. Leftover potatoes and a hot oven are all you need. Plus, there's no need to stand over a hot pan, flipping and frying individual hash brown rounds. The only trick to this recipe is to use well-chilled potatoes. If they are at all warm they will not grate properly.

Serves

4 to 6

3 to 4 medium-sized boiled or baked potatoes, cooled and chilled

3 tbsp (42 g) ghee, lard or coconut oil

¾ tsp sea salt

Preheat the oven to 425°F (220°C). Line a baking sheet with parchment paper. Shred the potatoes into 4 loosely packed cups (800 g). (I like to do this directly on the parchment paper.)

Sprinkle the ghee and salt over the potatoes and toss gently with 2 forks to combine. Place the pan in the middle of your oven and bake for 20 minutes, toss again with the forks and bake for an additional 25 to 30 minutes, for a total of 45 to 50 minutes, or until the potatoes are crispy and browned on the bottom and firm and lightly crisped in the middle.

Scientifically-Proven Method for Removing Pesticides

When you can't buy organic produce, there is a simple method that has been shown in studies to remove the most pesticides. This isn't to say we should stop purchasing organic foods. No, the foods on the Dirty Dozen list are often those whose pesticides reside deep within their core and cannot be washed off with a simple water solution.

In my opinion, this method is best for conventional produce on the Clean Fifteen list, or at the very least for those foods not on the Dirty Dozen list. It removes the pesticides from the surface of the produce, mostly. You cannot suck it from the middle of the fruit or vegetable.

This method involves two simple ingredients: baking soda and water. Fill a bowl or clean sink with water and add a teaspoon or so of baking soda. Stir that around and add your fruits and vegetables. Move them around in the water, rubbing the surface of the produce. Then, rinse really, really well under running water.

Curiously Delicious Cabbage Salad

One of the most economical vegetables to use is the common cabbage. We use it cooked in soups, stews and stir-fries as well as roasted, many recipes for which you'll find on these pages. But it also makes for a great salad—beyond coleslaw. Although cabbage salad can be admittedly bland, this one is not. The combination of flavors and textures come together to make a great side dish or, topped with a protein, a complete meal.

Serves
6

1 large head green cabbage (about 2 lb [905 g])

1 bunch green onions

1 bunch parsley

3 cloves garlic

2 large carrots

Juice of 2 lemons

¼ cup (60 g) tahini

2 tbsp (30 ml) apple cider vinegar

¼ cup (60 ml) olive oil

1 tsp sea salt, plus more as needed

⅓ cup (47 g) toasted sunflower seeds (see page 140)

Sprouted or Soaked Chickpea Falafel (page 47), Kidney Bean–Potato Patties (page 51) or your favorite protein, for serving

Shred the cabbage finely and place in a large salad bowl. Chop the green onions and parsley finely and add them to the cabbage. Finely mince the garlic and shred the carrots and add those to the salad bowl. Mix together all of the vegetables really well, using salad tongs or 2 forks.

In a pint-sized (500-ml) jar, combine the lemon juice, tahini, vinegar and olive oil. Season it with the salt. Seal the jar and shake vigorously. Pour the dressing over the salad, sprinkle with the sunflower seeds and mix well. Taste for salt and adjust as needed.

This is best left for at least 20 minutes before serving, to allow flavors to meld. Serve as a side salad or top with Sprouted or Soaked Chickpea Falafel (page 47), Kidney Bean–Potato Patties (page 51) or your favorite protein for a main dish salad.

Green Herb Sauce

This versatile sauce is great to have in your back pocket to serve over steamed potatoes or vegetables, on top of salads or over Sprouted or Soaked Chickpea Falafel (page 47). We use whatever fresh herbs we have on hand, in various combinations, and blend it up with just enough water to make it as thick or thin as we want it. Any way we make it, this sauce is always a delicious addition to a meal.

Makes
2 cups (475 ml) sauce

1 large avocado

2 large handfuls of any of the following: cilantro, parsley or basil, washed

2 cloves garlic, peeled

2 tbsp (30 ml) apple cider vinegar

¼ tsp red pepper flakes

Water, to thin

1½ tsp (9 g) salt, plus more as needed

Place the avocado, herbs, garlic, vinegar, red pepper flakes and water in a blender or food processor and blend. Taste and add salt, as needed.

Spanish Quinoa

Eating flavorful Spanish cuisine doesn't have to break the bank . . . nor does it have to always be rice and beans. Soaking quinoa and then using it as the base of this flavorful side dish gives me one more high-protein option for taco (or taco salad) night.

Serves
6

2¼ cups (389 g) raw quinoa

1 medium-sized onion, diced

2 tbsp (28 g) lard, coconut oil or ghee

1 tbsp (8 g) chili powder

2 tsp (12 g) salt

3 cups (710 ml) Bone Broth (page 150)

1 (15-oz [425-g]) can tomato sauce

1 (15-oz [425-g]) can diced tomatoes

Place the quinoa in a quart-sized (1-L) jar and fill the jar with filtered water. Stir the quinoa and water together and cover the jar. Leave to soak for 12 to 48 hours. Before proceeding with the recipe, drain and rinse the quinoa well.

In a 3-quart (2.8-L) saucepan, fry the onion in the lard over medium heat. Add the quinoa, chili powder, salt, broth, tomato sauce and diced tomatoes. Cover and bring to a boil. Lower the heat to a simmer and allow to cook, covered, for 15 to 20 minutes, or until the quinoa is completely cooked. Turn off the heat.

Leave the quinoa to rest for 5 minutes before fluffing and serving.

Szechuan Vegetables

I am almost certain that the ingredients in this recipe are not authentic to Szechuan cuisine, but we love the flavor and Asian cuisine inspiration. Tangy, slightly sweet and with just the right amount of kick, these veggies are one of my personal favorite means of eating a big plate of green.

Serves
4 to 6

¼ cup (55 g) coconut oil, lard or ghee

2 lb (905 g) asparagus, green beans, zucchini slices, carrot slices and/or sliced bell pepper

1 onion, thinly sliced

4 cloves garlic, minced

2 tbsp (30 g) tahini

1 tbsp (20 g) raw honey

1 tbsp (15 ml) apple cider vinegar

½ tsp ground ginger

½ cup (120 ml) Bone Broth (page 150)

½ tsp red pepper flakes

Salt, to taste

Roast chicken with rice or Crispy Oven-Baked Salmon Burgers (page 78), for serving

In a large skillet or wok over high heat, melt the coconut oil. Add the vegetables and onion and stir-fry for 3 to 5 minutes, or until they are just starting to soften but are still crisp.

Meanwhile, combine the garlic, tahini, honey, vinegar, ginger, broth, red pepper flakes and salt in a pint-sized (500-ml) jar. Seal the jar and shake well. Pour this mixture over the vegetables and cook for an additional 2 to 3 minutes, or until the sauce is just thickened and the vegetables are crisp-tender.

Serve alongside a roast chicken with rice or Crispy Oven-Baked Salmon Burgers (page 78).

Favorite Roasted Vegetables

I thought I hated Brussels sprouts, until I found out that you could roast them. This method for cooking vegetables has never once failed me, for every picky eater and every potentially offending vegetable. Without fail, every picky vegetable eater in our home will eat broccoli, cauliflower, Brussels sprouts, asparagus, cabbage, turnips and root vegetables . . . as long as I roast them. With their crispy edges and salty goodness, they're not a far cry from a French fry, really. And that's why we all love them and eat them often.

Serves
4 to 6

2 lb (905 g) any vegetables (see headnote)

¼ cup (60 ml) melted coconut oil, lard or ghee

1 tsp sea salt

½ tsp red pepper flakes (optional)

Preheat the oven to 425°F (220°C).

Prepare the vegetables by trimming the cauliflower or broccoli stalks, Brussels sprout stems, woody asparagus ends or tips and tails of root vegetables. Shred the cabbage or chop the vegetables into pieces no larger than 1 inch (2.5 cm).

Divide the vegetables between 2 sheet pans, pour the coconut oil over them and sprinkle them with the salt and red pepper flakes (if using).

Roast in the oven, rotating the pans after about 10 minutes for even browning, for 20 to 30 minutes, or until tender and browned around the edges.

Tomato Rice

This side dish comes together in a jiffy, with no chopping whatsoever. But the tomato sauce, coconut oil and spices give this side dish something special, taking the usual rice and beans to a whole new level. Use a thick-bottomed pot for this dish to prevent scorching.

Serves

4 to 6

3 tbsp (42 g) coconut oil, ghee or lard

2½ cups (488 g) uncooked jasmine rice

1 tsp chili powder

1 tsp ground cumin

3½ cups (830 ml) Bone Broth (page 150) or water

1 (15-oz [425-g]) can tomato sauce

2 tsp (12 g) salt

In an 8-quart (7.6-L) saucepan over medium-high heat, melt the coconut oil. Add the rice, chili powder and cumin and sauté for 2 to 3 minutes, or until toasted and fragrant. Pour in the broth, tomato sauce and salt, and stir to combine.

Bring to a boil, lower the heat to low and simmer, covered, for 15 to 20 minutes or until all the liquid is absorbed. Turn off the heat. Let sit, covered, for 5 more minutes before fluffing and serving.

On Arsenic & Rice

A staple grain for many cultures, rice has a rich history of use, both in its whole and refined forms, for generations. It follows, therefore, that rice can easily be considered a traditional food. That is why you will see it used as a staple gluten-free starch in this book and why our family is comfortable eating both forms of the grain.

But in recent years, concern has come to light over the level of arsenic in rice. With this discovery, modern laboratory testing has given us insight into a potential danger to our health. Several questions arise from these findings: Where is the arsenic coming from? Is it only in recent history that rice has been found to contain arsenic? Isn't arsenic naturally occurring? Should we just avoid rice altogether, then?

Let's take these one at a time.

First, the arsenic found in rice is thought to be coming from the water and soil the rice is grown in. Arsenic is a naturally occurring mineral found at various levels in drinking water and soils around the world. In very minute amounts, this mineral is considered acceptable. But the amounts found in rice are not minute. And the concentrations at which they are being found points to arsenic coming in larger quantities from an outside source, namely pesticides, herbicides and fertilizers.

It is likely that rice has long contained some level of arsenic. This is due to the fact that rice is generally grown throughout the world in what are called paddies—a flooded piece of land. The high-water method for growing rice naturally results in whatever substrates that are in the water being absorbed into the plant and therefore the grain. But again, these levels would be fairly minimal . . . unless they begin to receive water from an upstream location where arsenic may be in higher concentrations.

The most disturbing part of this equation is that arsenic is not something easily removed from the soil. So, even organic farming practices do not mean that arsenic will not be present. On the contrary, testing has shown organic varieties to contain just as much, if not more, than conventional brands.

So, what can we do?

First, be careful what rice you purchase. Rice grown in the southern part of the United States should be avoided completely. This area of the country is notorious for growing cotton, one of the most pesticide-heavy crops in the entire United States. All of that arsenic in the soil combined with the irrigation of rice paddies makes it the most arsenic-heavy rice in all of the testing that was done.

Studies show that rice sourced from California, India, Pakistan and Thailand seems to contain less arsenic. Likewise, jasmine and basmati varieties seem to be lower in arsenic.

Second, realize that arsenic is water soluble and can be significantly diminished through rinsing and proper cooking. Something practiced by many cultures who consume a lot of rice is a heavy rinsing of even white rice. Place the rice in plenty of water, stir and drain. Repeat the process a couple of times before cooking.

Brown rice, while higher in fiber, has been found to be higher in arsenic because it is stored in the bran. White rice is, therefore, a safer choice for avoiding arsenic.

Likewise, rice can be cooked in far more water than instructions generally call for. Two cups (390 g) of jasmine rice will often call for 3 cups (710 ml) of water. Try cooking it in 6 cups (1.4 L) of water instead, and once the cooking time is complete, pour off the excess water. The FDA has reported that the combination of rinsing and cooking in excess water can eliminate up to 50 to 60 percent of the arsenic present.

Finally, avoid baking with rice flour or purchasing gluten-free rice flour products. Rice flour has been, for years, the main flour present in the gluten-free baking world. But because rice is also one of our staple grains, and because rinsing and draining rice flour is much less viable an option, we choose to completely eliminate rice flour from our diet. You will notice that all the baked goods in this book utilize various other grains and flours.

With these tips, we feel we can safely continue to consume rice as a part of our daily diet.

Prudent Sweets & Treats

Oftentimes, it is the little things that make all the difference. Such is the case with eating traditional foods prepared on a budget: a little treat here, a sweetened drink there, and the sweet cravings are abated.

Actually, the impetus for this book was born out of a couple of recipes from this chapter combined with a few from the others. Just real food put together simply to create something surprisingly delicious, healthy enough to eat most every day.

When it comes to sweets and treats, I'm kind of a Scrooge. Not that I don't like to eat them, because I do. And not that I don't want my children to enjoy them, because I do. But I know what a daily intake of sugar—yes, even honey—can do to a body, and so I like to keep treats as, well, treats . . . something special you eat on occasion.

But even then, it has to be wholesome: good sweeteners, quality flours and fats, soaked grains, and always, always, it has to be homemade. Of course, it also has to be gluten-free and dairy-free and refined-sugar-free as well.

But that doesn't mean it can't be delicious . . . reminiscent of those favorite treats of my own youth, even. Cold, creamy shakes (pages 125 and 126); rich, dark chocolate cake (filled with a vegetable and no eggs, page 119); and even a nutrient-dense granola bar (page 123) to pack into a lunch box.

These are treats I am happy to feed to my family—snacks for the everyday and beverages we can give our children without the worry. And they are equal parts nourishing and delicious.

Dairy-Free Secret Ingredient Chocolate Pudding

Roasted sweet potatoes have a luscious and caramel-sweet filling when their jackets are removed. But what does that have to do with chocolate pudding? Well, a happy accident turned a buttery smooth side dish into one of our very favorite desserts that just so happens to be the epitome of rich, luscious chocolate pudding.

Makes
4 to 6 servings

2 medium-sized sweet potatoes

1 (13.5-oz [400-ml]) can coconut milk

½ cup (55 g) unsweetened cocoa powder

⅓ cup (115 g) honey, preferably raw

¼ tsp salt

½ tsp vanilla extract

Whipped cream or whipped coconut cream, for serving

Roast your sweet potatoes at 400°F (200°C) for about 50 minutes, or until completely tender and the bottoms are beginning to caramelize. Note: You can use leftover roasted sweet potatoes to make this quickly.

Remove the sweet potatoes from their jackets by peeling back the skins and scooping or squeezing out the flesh. Measure out 1 cup (240 g) of the sweet potato flesh and transfer to a blender. Add the coconut milk, cocoa powder, honey, salt and vanilla, and blend until very smooth. Blend for an additional 2 minutes to incorporate a little bit of air.

Pour into serving cups and refrigerate for at least 4 hours before serving. Serve with whipped cream or whipped coconut cream.

Chocolate Coconut Cream Pie with a Grain-Free Crust

I'm never one to run from chocolate or coconut. This pie really hits the spot on those special occasions. It is rich with good fats, not too sweet and fairly easy to throw together with a press-in crust. The macaroon-like crust can be used with all manner of fillings, so don't limit yourself to this filling. Refrigerating the pie will result in a more puddinglike consistency, whereas freezing will give you a firmer consistency.

Serves
8

Filling

1 (13.5-oz [400-ml]) can coconut milk, or 1½ cups (355 ml) homemade (page 136), at room temperature

¾ cup (83 g) unsweetened cocoa powder

¼ cup (55 g) coconut oil, melted

⅓ cup (75 g) coconut sugar or (115 g) honey, preferably raw

1 tsp vanilla extract

Pinch of salt

Crust

Coconut oil, for pan

2 cups (170 g) unsweetened shredded coconut

½ cup (64 g) tapioca starch

¼ tsp salt

¼ cup (60 ml) melted coconut oil

2 tbsp (40 g) honey, preferably raw

1 tsp vanilla extract

1 tbsp (15 ml) water

For the filling, in a blender, combine the coconut milk, cocoa powder, coconut oil, coconut sugar, vanilla and salt. Blend for 2 to 3 minutes, or until everything is well incorporated. Transfer the filling to the refrigerator and chill for at least 8 hours before proceeding with the crust. Alternatively, place in the freezer for 1½ to 2 hours and proceed with the crust.

For the crust, preheat the oven to 325°F (170°C) and oil a 10-inch (25-cm) pie pan with coconut oil.

In a medium-sized bowl, combine the coconut, tapioca starch and salt. Add the coconut oil, honey, vanilla and water, and mix well to incorporate. Transfer the crust mixture to the prepared pan and press it into the pan, covering the bottom and edges and forming a neat edge with your fingertips. Be sure to really press the mixture into the pan so that it holds together. Bake for 15 to 20 minutes, or until the crust is starting to turn golden around the edges and is set on the bottom. Allow the crust to cool completely before filling.

Carefully pour the filling into the baked and cooled piecrust and refrigerate for at least 6 hours before serving.

Soaked Chocolate Chunk Cookies

Everyone needs a good chocolate chip cookie recipe, right? Well, my definition of a good chocolate chip cookie has changed over the years. No longer do I enjoy its being cloyingly sweet, but a cookie with some chew to it is still a must. Chocolate chips we can live without, but good dark chocolate certainly has its place. And yes, butter is nice, but coconut oil can also produce a rich, buttery cookie. This unicorn of a recipe is the classic made a little healthier.

Makes
24 cookies

½ cup (112 g) coconut oil, softened, plus more for pan, if desired

2 tbsp (30 ml) Milk Kefir (page 146), or 1 tbsp (15 ml) coconut milk + 1 tbsp (15 ml) apple cider vinegar

1 cup (138 g) sorghum flour

½ cup (64 g) tapioca starch

1 tbsp (10 g) chia seeds

1 tbsp (4 g) ground psyllium husk

2 large, pasture-raised eggs

½ cup (113 g) coconut sugar

1 tsp vanilla extract

½ tsp sea salt

½ cup (88 g) 70% or darker chocolate chunks

½ tsp baking soda

In a medium-sized mixing bowl, beat together the coconut oil and kefir. In a separate bowl, whisk together the sorghum flour, tapioca starch, chia and psyllium. Add the dry ingredients to the coconut oil mixture and mix until a stiff dough forms. Cover and allow to soak for 8 to 12 hours.

Preheat the oven to 375°F (170°C). Grease a baking sheet with coconut oil or line it with parchment paper.

Crack the eggs into a small bowl and whisk. Whisk in the coconut sugar, vanilla and salt. Uncover the soaked dough, add the egg mixture and beat with a wooden spoon until everything comes together. Sprinkle the chocolate chunks and baking soda over the dough and mix well to combine.

Drop about 2 tablespoons (30 g) of dough per cookie 1½ inches (4 cm) apart onto the prepared baking sheet. Bake for 10 to 12 minutes, or until the cookies are just set and beginning to turn golden brown.

Remove from the oven and allow to cool on the pan for 5 minutes before transferring to a wire rack. Allow the cookies to cool completely before serving.

Sweet Potato Chocolate Cake *(egg-free)*

If you are not familiar with using buckwheat flour with chocolate, this cake will come as a pleasant surprise. Buckwheat has a distinctively nutty flavor that plays well with the bitterness of chocolate and excels in a cake recipe in which the flour is first soaked. Add to that a good serving of sweet potatoes, and this egg-free, dairy-free, gluten-free chocolate cake is a wholesome treat the whole family can enjoy.

Makes
12 slices

1¼ cups (295 ml) water

1 tbsp (15 ml) apple cider vinegar

1¾ cups (210 g) light buckwheat flour (no black flecks)

2 medium-sized sweet potatoes (about 12 oz [340 g])

2 tbsp (28 g) coconut oil, for pan

1¼ cups (283 g) coconut sugar

1 cup (111 g) unsweetened cocoa powder

1¼ tsp (7 g) salt

½ cup (120 ml) melted coconut oil

1 tsp vanilla extract

3.5 oz (99 g) 75% dark chocolate, melted in a double boiler (optional)

In a small bowl mix together the water and vinegar. In a medium-sized bowl, combine the buckwheat flour and vinegar mixture and whisk well. Cover and leave to soak for 12 to 24 hours.

Roast or steam the sweet potatoes. Once cool enough to handle, scrape out the flesh and blend into a thick puree, using a blender or food processor, and measure out 2 cups (480 g) to use in this recipe.

When the soaking period is up, preheat the oven to 350°F (180°C) and oil a 9 x 13–inch (23 x 33–cm) glass baking pan with the coconut oil. Uncover the soaking buckwheat flour and add the sweet potato puree, coconut sugar, cocoa powder, salt, melted coconut oil and vanilla. Stir everything together until well combined.

Scrape the batter into the prepared pan. Bake for 30 to 35 minutes, or until just set in the center when tested with a cake tester.

Remove from the oven and allow to cool completely in the pan before slicing and serving. Drizzle with melted chocolate, if desired.

ACV Apple Cider

Apple cider vinegar is a staple in our home; I use it nearly every day in everything from salads to beverages. This recipe is a juice–free replacement for that cinnamon–spiked quintessential fall beverage. Just a few simple ingredients are warmed carefully to protect the beneficial microorganisms in both the honey and vinegar.

Serves

4

1 qt (946 ml) water

⅓ cup (80 ml) apple cider vinegar

⅓ cup (115 g) honey, preferably raw

2 tsp (5 g) ground cinnamon

In a medium-sized saucepan, combine the water, vinegar, honey and cinnamon, and place over medium heat. Heat slowly, whisking a couple of times, until the mixture is warm to the touch but not so hot that you can't place a clean finger in it without feeling as though you will get burned, about 3 to 5 minutes.

Salty-Sweet Soaked Granola Bars

This is a riff off the granola in the first chapter (page 18). Baked up into one big pan and then sliced, this treat is a great grab-and-go snack. Soak it a little longer for a slight tang and you'll have a salty, sweet treat. To make it easy, this is essentially the granola recipe halved, so double the oats, chia seeds, kefir and seeds for the soaking step and then veer off into making both granola cereal and these granola bars.

Makes
16 bars

4½ cups (360 g) rolled oats, gluten-free, if needed

½ cup (80 g) chia seeds

1¼ cups (295 ml) Milk Kefir (page 146)

1½ cups (218 g) raw sunflower seeds or any combination of whole, raw seeds or nuts

2 tsp (12 g) sea salt for bars, plus 1 tsp for soaking

Coconut oil, for pan

½ cup (120 ml) melted coconut oil or unsalted butter

½ cup (170 g) honey, preferably raw

1½ cups (128 g) unsweetened shredded coconut

1½ tsp (8 ml) vanilla extract

1 cup add-ins, such as (175 g) chocolate chips or (150 g) dried fruit (optional)

A full 24 hours before you plan to bake the granola bars, in a large bowl, stir together the oats and chia seeds until evenly distributed. Pour in the milk kefir and mix, first with a wooden spoon and then with your hands, until all the oats and chia are moistened by the kefir. The mixture will not be terribly wet, but there will be a bit of moisture so that everything gets enough contact with the kefir for fermentation.

Cover the bowl with a lid or plastic wrap and leave to soak in a warm place in your kitchen for at least 24 hours. You can go as long as 48 hours for a bit more tang. Don't worry if, at the end of the soaking time, a very light white yeast begins to form on the surface; this is called kahm yeast and it is common in fermented foods like kefir.

Place the sunflower seeds in a quart-sized (1-L) jar, cover with water and add 1 teaspoon of the salt. Leave to soak for the duration of the oat-soaking period.

Once the oat-soaking period is up, preheat the oven to 325°F (170°C). Generously oil a half sheet baking pan with coconut oil.

Uncover the soaking oat mixture; it will be quite stiff, having absorbed all the liquid. Break it up into clumps with a sturdy wooden spoon. Drain the sunflower seeds very well (discard the salted water) and then add them to the broken-up oat mixture. Add the coconut oil, honey, shredded coconut, vanilla and salt, and mix everything together really well so that it is evenly distributed.

Transfer this mixture to your prepared pan and press it down evenly throughout the pan. Be firm in pressing it all down; this is what helps the granola bars stick together.

Bake for 35 to 40 minutes, or until lightly golden brown and firm.

Remove from the oven and allow to cool in the pan completely before slicing and removing.

Spiced Turmeric Chai Tea

I have combined two of our favorite teas in one with this beverage. This drink is full of great antioxidant-rich spices and has the perk of being caffeine-free since the base is raw honey and spices rather than tea. You can add more honey, if you like it supersweet, but to us this is just the right balance of comforting warm, well-spiced and gently sweetened.

Serves
8

¹/₃ cup (115 g) raw honey

1 tbsp (7 g) ground turmeric

¼ tsp freshly ground black pepper

½ tsp ground ginger

1 tsp ground cinnamon

¼ tsp ground cardamom

¼ tsp ground cloves

6 cups (1.4 L) water

2 cups (475 ml) coconut milk

In a small bowl, combine the honey, turmeric, pepper, ginger, cinnamon, cardamom and cloves. Divide this mixture equally among 4 mugs. Heat the water gently until it is warm to the touch but not hot enough to burn. Pour the water into the mugs and stir well. Divide the coconut milk among the 4 mugs and serve.

Real Food Frosty

If you grew up with a Wendy's nearby, you know exactly what a Frosty is. If not, know that it is similar to a milk shake, but with a very distinct flavor and texture somewhere between vanilla and chocolate. It is thick and creamy and the perfect cold treat for a hot day. This recipe is a re-creation of that thick fast-food shake, but cleaned up a lot. Egg yolks work to emulsify the ingredients into one thick shake that you don't have to buy ice cream to make.

Serves
4

1 (13.5-oz [400-ml]) can full-fat coconut milk, or 1½ cups (355 ml) homemade (page 136)

1½ cups (355 ml) water, divided

⅓ cup (37 g) unsweetened cocoa powder

¼ cup (85 g) honey, preferably raw (see notes)

1 tsp vanilla extract

4 large, pasture-raised egg yolks (see Notes)

In a small saucepan, combine the coconut milk and ½ cup (120 ml) of the water over medium heat. Add the cocoa powder and heat, whisking constantly, until the cocoa powder has dissolved. Remove from the heat and set aside to cool.

Once the coconut milk mixture is nearing room temperature, add the honey and whisk really well until everything is combined. Pour the mixture into an ice cube tray and freeze until completely solid.

Once the ice cubes are frozen, place them in a blender. Add the vanilla, egg yolks and the remaining 1 cup (240 ml) of water, and blend until completely smooth. Serve ice cold.

Notes: You can replace the honey with coconut sugar, but be sure to add it with the cocoa powder while the milk mixture is hot, so that it has a chance to dissolve.

Be very careful with your choice of egg yolks. I only use our homegrown pasture-raised eggs when consuming them raw and I recommend that you at least know that your farmer has clean, sustainable practices before consuming raw eggs.

Creamy Raspberry Milk Shake

Rich, cold, sweet and delicious; this shake is far greater than the sum of its parts. It works well with strawberries or blueberries, but there is something about the tang of the raspberries coupled with fragrant vanilla and rich coconut milk that makes it taste like, well, a real-deal milk shake.

Serves
2

1 (13.5-oz [400-ml]) can coconut milk, or 1½ cups (355 ml) homemade (page 136)

1 cup (250 g) frozen raspberries

½ tsp vanilla extract

2 large, pasture-raised egg yolks (optional)

1½ tbsp (30 g) raw honey, plus more to taste

Place the coconut milk in the refrigerator at least 12 hours before assembling the shake.

In a blender, combine the chilled coconut milk, raspberries, vanilla, egg yolks (if using) and honey, and blend until completely smooth. Taste and add additional honey, if desired. Serve immediately.

Raw or Dairy-Free Mexican Sipping Chocolate

The captivating flavor combination of this thick, rich drinking chocolate is hard to explain, but it works magnificently. It is complex from the flavors of the corn and the spices, but simultaneously familiar from the creamy chocolate. You really must try it for yourself to understand how good it is.

Serves
4 to 6

½ cup (56 g) masa flour

2 cups (475 ml) water

½ cup (56 g) unsweetened cocoa powder

⅓ cup (75 g) coconut sugar (if using milk) or (115 g) honey, preferably raw

¼ tsp ground cinnamon

Pinch of cayenne pepper (optional)

Pinch of sea salt

2 cups (475 ml) raw milk, or 1 (15-oz [444-ml]) can full-fat coconut milk

Place the masa flour in a medium-sized saucepan over medium heat. Slowly stream in the water, whisking constantly to avoid lumps. Bring the masa mixture to a simmer and whisk in the cocoa powder, coconut sugar (if using), cinnamon, cayenne (if using) and salt.

If using coconut milk, whisk in the coconut milk and raw honey. If using raw milk, remove the pan from the heat and allow it to cool until you can comfortably dip a clean finger into the mixture without it feeling too hot. Whisk in the raw milk until everything is homogenous.

Serve warm in mugs.

Penny-Pinching DIYs

Paying other people to make stuff for you is both convenient and expensive. It's not always a pleasant truth, but truth it is. As a newlywed, I realized this when I learned that one can make one's own yogurt. I stood in the dairy aisle staring at a $3 quart (L) of yogurt and then at a $5 gallon (4 L) of milk. It saves to do it yourself.

A few things that we make ourselves really cut down on the budget: broths and sprouts, the best homemade corn tortillas and coconut milk, dairy-free cheese sauce and sunflower seed butter. But not only are these saving us money, they are simply so good homemade that you can't buy a comparable counterpart in the grocery store.

I will admit, I am stubborn when it comes to this topic. If it's expensive, I'm making it myself or we're doing without. You can make kombucha yourself for pennies on the dollar. Coconut milk costs at least 30 percent less when you blend it up yourself. And don't even get me started on what it costs to purchase two-ingredient bone broth if you're not willing to make it yourself.

The good news is that these are not huge time commitments. And oftentimes, I pick my battles. Homemade bone broth is going to save me more than homemade coconut milk, so I buy a lot of coconut milk. I also try to think about the fact that I would be hard-pressed to even find cultured oat yogurt or sprouted beans at my local grocery store.

I hope these recipes become what they have for me: tools you can pull out of your back pocket. Some come out weekly, such as broth and corn tortillas. Others are more occasional, like sunflower seed butter and cheese sauce. But all of them save us money and taste better than any overpriced thing I could buy at a grocery store. Perhaps they will do the same for you.

Homemade Cultured Oatgurt

Fermented grains aren't just for making bread or porridge, although this ferment works well for the latter. This fermented oat mixture, blended up, was created to stand in for dairy-based yogurt or kefir. This recipe easily doubles or triples for a larger batch.

Makes
about 3 cups (690 g)

2 cups (160 g) rolled oats, gluten-free, if needed

1¾ cups (414 ml) water

1 tbsp (15 ml) culture starter, kefir, whey or kombucha

In a quart-sized (1-L) jar, combine the oats, water and culture starter. Stir well and cover the jar with a permeable lid, such as a clean cloth, paper towel or coffee filter. Set in a warm, draft-free area of your kitchen. Leave to ferment for 24 to 48 hours.

When ready to serve, you can make something the consistency of either buttermilk or yogurt. In either case, first transfer a spoonful of the oats and soaking liquid to a new quart-sized (1-L) jar. Feed that mixture more oats and water and you'll have another batch within another day or two.

For buttermilk-consistency oatgurt, simply take the contents of the original jar and blend it using either an immersion or a countertop blender. For more of a yogurt thickness, pour the contents of the jar through a sieve and let most of the water run out. Then, blend this into a thick, yogurtlike paste.

Use the thinner oatgurt in smoothies, baking, salad dressings or to soak whole grains. Use the thicker oatgurt as a yogurt substitute in bowls with fruit, nuts, granola and so on.

Broth-Based Dairy-Free Cheese Sauce

If you are dairy-free, one of the things you may miss the most is cheese—on broccoli, nachos, beans, and really, all the Mexican foods you have always wanted to make more nourishing. This sauce is my answer to that dilemma. A few vegetables, broth and spices come together to form a sauce perfect for dipping or topping your favorite meals.

Makes
3½ cups (828 ml)

1½ cups (165 g) peeled and diced potato

½ cup (65 g) sliced carrot

1 cup (240 ml) Bone Broth (page 150)

¼ cup (55 g) coconut oil, melted

⅓ cup (43 g) nutritional yeast

2 tsp (12 g) sea salt, plus more as needed

¾ tsp garlic powder

½ jalapeño pepper, seeded and diced

1 tbsp (15 ml) apple cider vinegar

½ tsp ground cumin

Pinch of ground turmeric

In a medium-sized saucepan, combine the potatoes and carrots, and cover with water. Simmer over medium heat for about 10 minutes, or until they are completely tender. Drain off the cooking water.

If using a countertop blender, transfer the cooked vegetables to the blender and add the broth, coconut oil, nutritional yeast, salt, garlic powder, jalapeño, vinegar, cumin and turmeric. If using an immersion blender, add all the remaining ingredients to the saucepan and blend. Taste and adjust the salt, as needed.

Homemade Coconut Milk *(for less)*

You don't have to have a high-powered blender to make this drink, though it certainly helps. I make it with our immersion blender and we end up with a quart (1-L) of coconut milk that's just a little less rich than the store-bought full-fat counterparts. From my rough calculations, this saves us at least 30 percent off the cheapest cans of coconut milk available in the store.

Makes
1 quart (1 L)

2 cups (170 g) unsweetened shredded coconut

4 cups (946 ml) water

Place the coconut in a ½-gallon-sized (2-L) heatproof jar.

Bring the water to a boil, then carefully pour it over the shredded coconut. Stir the water and coconut, cover the jar and leave it to sit for 1 to 2 hours, or until relatively cool.

Blend the coconut and water, using an immersion blender, or transfer the mixture to a countertop blender and blend for 3 to 4 minutes.

Place a nut milk bag or a fine strainer over a wide bowl or 2-quart (2-L) measuring cup. Pour the contents of the jar through the nut milk bag or strainer. Wring or press the coconut pulp several times, until it seems fully dry, to extract all the milk.

Transfer the milk to a quart-sized (1-L) jar and use right away or store in the refrigerator for up to a week. You'll have to shake the milk well before serving, as it does not contain the binders the store-bought brands often do.

The Best Gluten-Free Bone Broth Gravy

Having broth in the house means you can make one of the most delicious—and frugal!—foods I know of: gravy. We will brown just a tiny bit of meat and make it right in the pan to use up all those drippings or keep it simple by omitting the meat. And don't feel you have to just serve it over potatoes or rice, though those are frugal options as well. If you are controlling your carbs, try serving it over steamed broccoli, roasted Brussels sprouts (see Favorite Roasted Vegetables, page 105) or sautéed cabbage. It'll stretch out a tiny portion of meat or stand in for the protein altogether.

Makes
8 cups (1.9 L)

8 oz (225 g) ground beef or leftover cooked chicken (optional)

2 qt (1.9 L) Bone Broth (page 150)

3 tbsp (27 g) potato starch

⅓ cup (80 ml) water

I tsp onion powder (optional)

½ tsp freshly ground black pepper

Salt

If you are adding meat to the gravy, in a large skillet, brown it over high heat and then transfer it to a plate. Add the broth to the skillet and bring to a boil, scraping the bottom of the pan to loosen the extra bits of meat and pan drippings.

If not adding meat, in a medium-sized saucepan, bring the broth to a boil. Lower the heat to low and allow the broth to simmer for 5 minutes to partially reduce. Meanwhile, combine the potato starch with the water in a pint-sized (500-ml) jar. Whisk really well to make a slurry.

Once the broth has simmered for 5 minutes, slowly pour the potato starch slurry into the broth while whisking constantly. Cook for just a couple of minutes, whisking constantly, until the gravy has thickened. Turn off the heat.

Season the gravy with the onion powder (if using), pepper and salt, as desired. If your gravy tastes bland or flavorless, it needs more salt. Serve hot. Any leftovers can be transferred to a glass jar and refrigerated for up to a week. Reheat very gently over low heat, just until warm, before serving.

Better Sunflower Seed Butter

It takes a high-powered blender or heavy-duty food processor to make a one-ingredient nut butter. Not owning either of those, I set out to make a butter from my favorite frugal seeds. I use an immersion blender to whiz this guy up and it is rich and delicious, the perfect replacement for all those expensive jars of nut and seed butters in the store. Plus, soaking the seeds makes them much easier on the belly.

Makes
1½ to 2 cups (390 to 520 g)

2 cups (290 g) raw sunflower seeds

¼ cup (55 g) expeller-pressed coconut oil

½ tsp sea salt

1 tbsp (20 g) honey, preferably raw (optional)

Place the seeds in a quart-sized (1-L) jar and fill with water up to the 3-cup (710-ml) mark. Cover loosely and let sit for 12 hours on your countertop.

The next day, preheat your oven to 300°F (150°C). Drain the seeds and rinse them.

Spread them thinly on a baking sheet and place them in the oven. Toast for 15 minutes. Remove the pan from the oven, stir the seeds around, then return the pan to the oven for an additional 10 minutes, or until they are dry and toasty.

Remove the seeds from the oven and allow to cool just enough to handle.

In a blender or a quart-sized (1-L) jar (if using an immersion blender), combine the toasted seeds with the coconut oil, salt and honey (if using). Pulse until a thick paste forms, then blend for 1 to 2 minutes, or until it is creamy and smooth. Serve as you would any nut or seed butter.

Store in the refrigerator for up to several weeks, but I doubt it will last that long.

How to Make Sunflower Sprouts

You can sprout all types of seeds, but one of the best to start with are sunflower seeds. They result in big, saladlike sprouts that you can use in all sorts of yummy ways. They're also substantially cheaper to sprout than many other seeds. If you've ever been intimidated by sprouting, please know it only takes minutes a day and results in one of the highest-enzyme foods you can consume.

One thing I do, since I am forgetful and distracted, is put my sprouting jars near my water source. We have a water filter, so I just leave my jars on the counter next to it. That way, when I go for a glass of water, I see them and spend about 2 minutes draining and rinsing them.

To sprout: Place 1 cup (145 g) of raw sunflower seeds in a quart-sized (1-L) jar. Cover with water and a breathable lid and leave to soak for 12 hours.

Drain and rinse the seeds and invert the jar in a bowl so that it lies at a 45-degree angle upside down. This helps any excess water drain from the seeds.

Rinse the seeds every 8 to 12 hours. A 12-hour window between rinsing will be fine if it is cooler. If it is 80°F (27°C) or warmer, rinsing at the 8-hour mark will help prevent any fermentation from occurring.

Continue the cycle of rinsing and draining for 2 to 4 days, or until little sprouts begin to form. You can now utilize these seeds with the baby sprouts for granolas, snacking, and so on, once you dehydrate them and halt the sprouting process.

For big sunflower sprouts for salads or other dishes, continue the sprouting process for an additional 2 to 3 days, or until the sprouts are 1 to 2 inches (2.5 to 5 cm) long. Rinse one last time and serve or refrigerate for several days.

How to Sprout Grains and Beans

When dealing with grains and beans, you can think of them as seeds because, in reality, that is what they are. The popular soaking method works well, especially for flour, but in dealing with whole grains and beans, sprouting goes a step further. It is as simple as soaking, rinsing and giving the seeds a bit of time. The grains and beans I have found to be the easiest to sprout are brown rice, buckwheat, quinoa, chickpeas and lentils.

Makes
3 cups (350 g) sprouted beans or grains

2 cups (350 to 400 g) dried grains or (400 g) dried beans

Water, as needed

Place the dried grains or seeds in a ½-gallon-sized (2-L) jar or similarly sized bowl. Add 6 cups (1.4 L) of water and allow to soak for 12 hours.

After 12 hours, drain and rinse the grains or beans. If using a half-gallon (2-L) jar, put a mesh sprouting screen over your lid and invert your jar in a bowl at a 45-degree angle. This will allow any remaining liquid to drain off. Allow to rest for 12 hours.

Continue this pattern of rinsing and draining followed by 12 hours of resting/inverted draining for 2 to 4 days, or until little shoots begin to emerge from your grains or beans.

When they first begin to sprout, you can consume the grains or beans as is, cooked as you normally would with about 25 percent less liquid needed in the cooking process. At this stage, the cooked grains and beans will have no tangible flavor difference from their unsprouted counterparts.

Continuing the sprouting process for another day or so will only enhance the benefits of the sprouting process. The sprouts will get a bit longer and their taste will change from that of a creamy, starchy grain or bean to more of a vegetable flavor.

(Continued)

How to Sprout Grains and Beans *(Continued)*

Troubleshooting:

Things can vary a lot in sprouting, because it is a living process and because variables are often different. Here are a couple of common problems:

My beans or grains aren't sprouting even though it's been days. Are your beans and grains organic? Sometimes the chemicals used in conventional agriculture can halt the process of sprouting. Are your beans or grains older? At some point, they lose their ability to sprout due to heat or age, just as a garden seed is only viable for a year or two under common circumstances.

My beans or grains have a slimy film on them when I rinse them. This is normal; it is the starches coming out of the seed and into the water. You might consider giving them a couple of rinses instead of just one, to remove all that starch.

My beans or grains are starting to stink/ferment. In my experience, this is almost always because it is too warm. The best way to prevent this is to rinse your grains or beans more frequently to remove the starches before they ferment. Two more rinses—every 4 hours or so—in a 12-hour period may be necessary in warmer weather.

I can't seem to rinse them thoroughly. If your jar or vessel is too crowded, you won't be able to get enough water to the surface area of the grain or bean and this can also cause fermentation. Divide your sprouts into more vessels as they grow, if needed, or just transfer them to a larger one.

How to Make Milk Kefir

Milk kefir is possibly one of my very favorite fermented foods. It is so very versatile in the kitchen and is widely considered one of the most beneficial fermented foods. Because it is a staple in our kitchen in everything from baked goods to smoothies, we make a half-gallon (2-L) batch nearly every single day. For Dairy-Free Milk Kefir, see Traditionally Fermented Foods.

Makes
1 quart (1 L) milk kefir, plus starter for additional batches

I tsp to I tbsp (6 to 18 g) milk kefir grains

I qt (I L) cleanest, freshest milk you can find (not ultrapasteurized)

In a quart-sized (1-L) jar, combine the milk kefir grains and the milk. Gently stir with a wooden spoon and cover with a permeable lid, such as a clean cloth, coffee filter or paper towel. Secure with a canning ring or rubber band.

Leave the jar to culture for 12 to 36 hours, or until it seems to have thickened into a curd. In warmer weather, 12 to 24 hours is sufficient; in cooler weather, 24 to 36 hours may be needed.

Place a canning funnel inside a clean quart-sized (1-L) jar and place a strainer atop the funnel. Pour the kefir through the strainer, stirring or tapping the strainer on the rim of the funnel, if needed, to help the kefir pass through the strainer while the grains remain.

Transfer the grains to a fresh quart (1 L) of milk and repeat the culturing process for successive batches of kefir.

Use or consume your kefir straight away or store it in the refrigerator for I to 2 weeks.

Easy & Traditional Homemade Corn Tortillas

While they may not seem like a big deal, corn tortillas generally fall into three categories: bland, tough store-bought varieties; okay homemade tortillas made from the directions on the back of a bag of masa flour; and toasty, soft, delicious fresh tortillas cooked traditionally. You don't have to soak and grind your own corn for the latter, but you do need to know the method I learned from watching women from such countries as Nicaragua and Costa Rica make the tortillas with the method that they and their foremothers have used for generations. The most important tip is that a tortilla has three sides. That may seem impossible and, technically speaking, there really are only two sides. But, when you flip the tortilla to cook on that "third side" you're really just finishing the cooking of the tortilla's first side in a way that allows the tortilla to puff beautifully.

Serves
4 to 6

Up to 1¾ cups (414 ml) water, divided

2 cups (224 g) organic masa flour

½ tsp sea salt

Heat all the water until nearly boiling. In a medium-sized bowl, stir together the flour and salt. Pour 1½ cups (355 ml) of the water into the flour mixture and mix with a wooden spoon. The dough will start to hydrate, but will look pretty dry still. Set aside.

Place a 2-burner griddle or 2 skillets over medium-high heat and allow to heat for at least 5 minutes.

Using clean hands, knead the masa dough for a minute or two to gauge the moisture level. The final dough should be tacky and moist, but not sticky. You should be able to compress the dough in your hand and not find cracks around the edges. Add an additional 2 to 4 tablespoons (30 to 60 ml) of water to the dough and mix it in, if needed.

Line a tortilla press either with parchment paper or with a quart-sized (1-L) ziplock bag. Cut off the zipper part of the bag and then cut down both side seams to form a bag with one seam.

Once the griddle is preheated and the press lined, take about 3 tablespoons (45 g) of dough and form it into a tight ball in your hand. Put the ball into the middle of the lined press and gently press until the dough just begins to emerge from the edge of the press. Open the press and remove the tortilla. Carefully lay 1 edge of the tortilla down and gradually lay the rest of it down. (Note that if you just slap it down all at once, it often sticks and doesn't form the "seal" as it does if you lay it down gradually, end to end.)

(Continued)

Easy & Traditional Homemade Corn Tortillas (Continued)

Cook the first side of the tortilla for 15 to 20 seconds, or until it just starts to dry up around the edges and you can slip a spatula underneath. Flip and cook on the second side for 45 to 60 seconds, or until it has just started to brown and show some color. If it is still completely pale, cook for an additional 15 to 20 seconds before flipping to the "third" side (i.e., back to the first side).

This final side of cooking is done to let the tortilla puff up, which creates a very tender tortilla. Cook on this final side for up to 30 to 45 seconds, or until it has puffed up. If it doesn't puff up at first, check that what is now the top of the tortilla has some color to it. If not, flip it back over until it does. If it does have color and doesn't need to be flipped, gently press down on the tortilla until it starts to puff and move the spatula around to help it to puff all over.

Transfer to a platter and repeat with remaining tortillas.

Tortillas are best eaten fresh with soups, as a taco shell or with a simple pot of beans. They will keep for a few days, but are best the next day. When they are cool, wrap them up in a clean kitchen towel. To reheat, sprinkle them with a bit of water and reheat on a hot griddle for 15 to 20 seconds per side.

Bone Broth *(with a rare tip)*

Because broth is one of those two-ingredient simple methods for an age-old food, it almost seems silly to put a recipe for it in any cookbook. So, why do it? Well, there is one little nuance to the process that I have added that seems to help my broth gel better. I don't really know how it works but, after reading about it in an old cookbook and finding great results in my own kitchen, I was sold.

Makes
2 gallons (7.6 L)

4 lb (1.8 kg) beef, chicken, lamb or pork bones

2 gal (7.6 L) water

Herbs and/or vegetables

Place the bones in a pot and cover them with water. Add herbs and vegetables, as desired, to impart flavor and minerals. Bring to a boil and then lower the heat to very low. How low? Well, you should really only see little bubbles coming to the surface here and there; nothing like a rolling boil or even a simmer.

Once the heat is just right, cover the pot and leave to simmer for 12 hours for chicken broth or 24 hours for larger bones, such as beef, lamb or pork. Turn off the heat and let the pot sit for 12 hours to cool. If you're worried about bacteria, don't; you'll be boiling it before you are all finished.

After the cooling period, bring the broth to a simmer over high heat, turn off the heat and allow the broth to cool for at least 30 to 60 minutes, or until you are comfortable handling it. If you are making beef, lamb and to a smaller extent pork broth, you will want to make sure to pour the broth through the strainer (see next step) while it is hot, so that the fat doesn't solidify first. If you desire to completely remove the fat, let it cool completely, skim off the fat and then pour the broth through the strainer.

Place a strainer atop half-gallon or quart-sized (2- or 1-L) jars, set a strainer over the funnel and fill the jars with the broth, leaving a little extra headspace if freezing (see tips). Allow to cool before refrigerating.

Three Tips for Getting Broth into Your Family Every Day

If your family is like mine, not everyone wants soup or a steaming mug of broth every day. To remedy that—and make sure the littlest ones are regularly consuming broth—here are a few methods I use.

- Make really thick soups, like Sweet Potato & Beet Soup (page 48). I find picky eaters prefer this over a brothy soup.
- Cook all the grains and beans in broth rather than water; you'd be surprised how much broth you can sneak in.
- Make gravy (page 139) at least once or twice a week. Our whole family loves this stuff!

Four Tips for Safely Freezing Broth in Glass Jars

Freezing broth is a great way to preserve it, but I have had too many cracked jars over the years to think this is foolproof. There are a few things you can do to prevent your glass jars from cracking as the broth freezes and expands:

- Resist the urge to fill jars completely; instead, fill them 80 percent full.
- Wait until the broth is at room temperature before placing them in the freezer.
- Place the jars in the freezer without lids. Once they are frozen solid, place a lid on them.
- Don't let your jars touch in the freezer while they are freezing.

Once you have a freezer full of broth, a few more tips make storage and usage safe and foolproof.

- For one, be careful of how you move jars around. Glass can break more easily when under the stress of freezing temperatures.
- When defrosting, do not put the jars into hot water. Instead thaw slowly in the refrigerator or on the counter. For a slightly swifter method, place the jars in cool or room temperature water.

Resources

Where you shop can make a huge difference in how much you spend on any given food. With the options available to me, I have narrowed down where I can get the best price per unit or pound. You can find an exhaustive list on the Nourishing Days blog, but what follows is the general breakdown.

Azure Standard

- Gluten-free flours
- Gluten-free grains
- Beans
- Sunflower & chia seeds
- Expeller-pressed coconut oil
- Himalayan pink salt
- Avocado & olive oil
- Bulk spices
- 50-pound (22.7-kg) bags of organic potatoes on sale

Amazon

- Bulk tahini

Walmart

- Rice
- Organic coffee
- Frozen wild blueberries
- Organic carrots
- Frozen kale
- Frozen green beans

Aldi

- Avocados
- Coconut milk cans
- Conventional produce
- Occasionally organic produce
- Grass-fed beef
- Wild Alaskan salmon (canned and frozen)
- Frozen broccoli
- Paper products
- Canned tomatoes and tomato products (conventional & organic)
- Garlic & onions
- Sweet potatoes

Acknowledgments

A book such as this is born over years rather than the short months in which it is finally written. The recipes contained in this book are, by and large, the product of finding ways to feed my growing family nourishing, mostly organic foods without breaking the bank. They came from a quick lunch thrown together with potatoes and beans or a staple breakfast we all loved so I made it over and over. First and foremost, therefore, I'd like to thank my husband, Stewart, and my children for trying the oh-so-many experiments throughout the years and for being honest when they weren't so great (those didn't make the cut).

To my oldest sons, thank you for being such hard working and therefore very hungry (all the time) boys. Keeping you full has been a challenge, but one I gladly accept and am grateful to be a part of.

To my two biggest girls, thank you for all of your help and enthusiasm in the kitchen. So many of these recipes literally had your hands right in them and it is beyond a pleasure to work alongside you, see you smile at the results and watch you snag bites as we go about our days.

To my babies, who have both sat on my hip while Mama has written a cookbook. What a gift it has been to carry you from counter to stove to photography setup and see your little pudgy fingers in all of it.

To Stewart, thank you for your love and support and so much help throughout this process, even while working so hard on everything else you do. It is a joy to be your wife.

To Page Street Publishing, for partnering with me once again on one of my favorite topics. To Marissa, for working with an unknown-to-you author and lending so much to the project. And to Will and the design team for the opportunity and talent you bring.

To our church family, for your prayers, babysitting help and the table that was gifted us that has graced most of the photos in this book. We are so very grateful for you all!

All glory be to the Lord Jesus Christ.

About the Author

Shannon Stonger is the creator of the blog Nourishing Days and has authored *100% Rye*, *Traditionally Fermented Foods* and co-authored *The Doable Off-Grid Homestead*. Alongside her husband, Stewart, and their six children, she lives on an off-grid homestead in Texas. She spends her days stretching the grocery budget while feeding and home-educating her young children, gardening, preserving and trying to clean up the messes from all the making.

Index

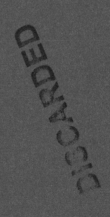
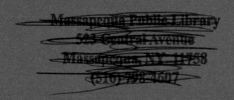